(handwritten inscription: "For (and now (and now) PART of that story flow, too). Katryn 11/23/19")

CROSS KEYS, CARPET BAG AND PEN

*Letters depicting three Ohio families
during the Civil War*

Letters Compiled and Edited with
Introductions by
Kathryn Hardgrove Popio

Otter Bay Books
BALTIMORE, MD 2018

Please direct all correspondence and book orders to:
Kathryn Hardgrove Popio
P. O. Box #1044
Norton, OH 44203

Schedule Kathryn Hardgrove Popio as speaker for your group.
Kathryn.Hardgrove.Popio@gmail.com

Library of Congress Control Number 2018935168
ISBN 978-0-692-08227-0

Published for the author by
Otter Bay Books, LLC
3507 Newland Road
Baltimore, MD 21218-2513

www.otter-bay-books.com

Printed in the United States of America

Dedicated to Earl Kulgoskie
with thanksgiving for
his meticulous work
to uncover Hardgrove stories
and nudge me to do the same.

CONTENTS

ACKNOWLEDGMENTS

I spent many hours driving the length and breadth of Lawrence and Massillon areas to imagine living "back in the day." Here are people who rewarded my quest to present these letters, with their plethora of details, in a way that may serve future researchers.

Massillon History: Massillon Museum archivist Mandy Altimus Stahl provided abundant resources in understanding Massillon's 19th century business leaders. Jill Ringer, Massillon Library's History Specialist, discovered details I could not find, and her "History Room" assistants, Christian, Jessica Watkins and Jessica Shoemaker, provided helpful microfilm support during my work there. I am also grateful for the invaluable assistance of Rose Buxton of the Massillon Cemetery office for record searches and for walking with me one summer morning to the grave site of Hannah (Justus) Hardgrove and little Willy.

Canal Fulton History: To Diana Drake and Betsy at Canal Fulton Library, thanks for setting out atlases and assisting with reference questions. Thanks to Robert Hodges, curator at the Canal Museum, for rich background of Canal Fulton's influence as prelude to my volunteer work there the season of 2016. A special thank you also to cousins Marvin and Wilma Hardgrove for taking a day to drive me through Lawrence Township to glean more gold nuggets of remembrances. Lastly, I enjoyed talking with Brian Graham and Tom Hardgrove about Canal Fulton's history.

Township Histories: Thanks to conversations with Susan Faber and Vern Wolgamott, I was enlightened of township boundaries and roads in once-vital small communities like North Lawrence, Newman and Youngstown. Dean Speicher shared background of Pigeon Run and Bonnie Knerr lent insight into Brookfield and also Tuscarawas Township. Thanks to Carol Blose at Lawrence Township offices and Linda Simon of Canal Fulton Heritage Society for checking into historical township ledgers and roads. I am also thankful for Mike Mahaney's historical research in which he documented locations of early land grant owners, pioneer contributions and cemetery records.

Historical Assistance in Canton: The Stark County Recorder's office and Jennie, in particular, offered great help with land searches. My thanks to Canton Public Library's history room staff for assistance in microfilm searches. Plus, it was a breathtaking moment when Kim Kenney, William McKinley Museum curator, brought out the Ferdinand Brader drawing of the George Hardgrove homestead on Butterbridge Road for me to drink in. To Mark Holland, archivist for William McKinley Presidential Library, and museum volunteer Tom Haas, my gratitude for Justus family and Civil War searches.

Wayne County History: To Pam Blaha, Deb Kitko, and Cheryl Abernathy of OGS, Wayne Chapter, thanks for opening avenues to all sorts of resources and answering questions about Hardgrove(s) in Wayne County, Ohio, and Washington County, Pennsylvania. Little did I know that my quest would soon lead me to Brewster, Sugarcreek Township Historical Society, where Robert Luckring provided background on the community of Justus. My gratitude to Shiela and Dave Schmidt for sending a copy of their Butterbridge family tree, which helped me sort out primary relationships. Thanks also that Mildred Schmidt of Orrville shared family letters with cousin Earl Kulgoski. Many thanks to Sherrie Stallsmith of Orrville Historical Society's museum and the staff, Georgene Wright and Judy Pouly. They graciously dug into photos revealing Orrville's thriving 1860s downtown. My thanks to Marcia Boston of Orrville Library who pulled their best histories for me to peruse.

Washington County, Pennsylvania: I appreciated the searches and input of Chuck Edgar, research assistant at the LeMoyne House of Washington, Pennsylvania, regarding John Crawford Hardgrove's background and War of 1812 experiences.

Mt. Vernon History: I was so grateful to Christie Smith of Mt. Vernon Public Library for supplying background on the tiny community of Jelloway, where William Hardgrove lived.

Special Thank You: To Carman Kulgoski, cousin Earl's wife, for her dedication to preserving his genealogical library and passing it on to me. To Minnie Hardgrove, who wrote about her beloved families and Butterbridge homestead—sometimes in notebooks and sometimes on brown paper bags. To Helen and Gary Strine for sharing Strine history. Finally, for critiques by my daughter, Heather Popio, which greatly helped round-out the central characters in the letters. To Phyllis Mahaney who was my sounding-board to book title alterations. Last, but not least, my gratitude to Ann Hughes and Kate Boyer at Otter Bay Books for mentoring my project. Their guidance was a huge blessing.

APPRECIATION FOR PHOTOGRAPHS & DRAWINGS

McKinley Presidential Library and Museum in Canton, Ohio
    (Permission to use Ferdinand Brader's rendition)

Massillon Museum collection in Massillon, Ohio
    (Permission to use photos of American House Hotel
        and Massillon Depot)

The Massillon Independent Newspaper
    (Permission to use image of O. J. Hardgrove's
    invention as it appeared on pages in 1865)

Massillon Public Library on Lincolnway in Massillon, Ohio
    (Electronic image of O. J. Hardgrove's Ad)

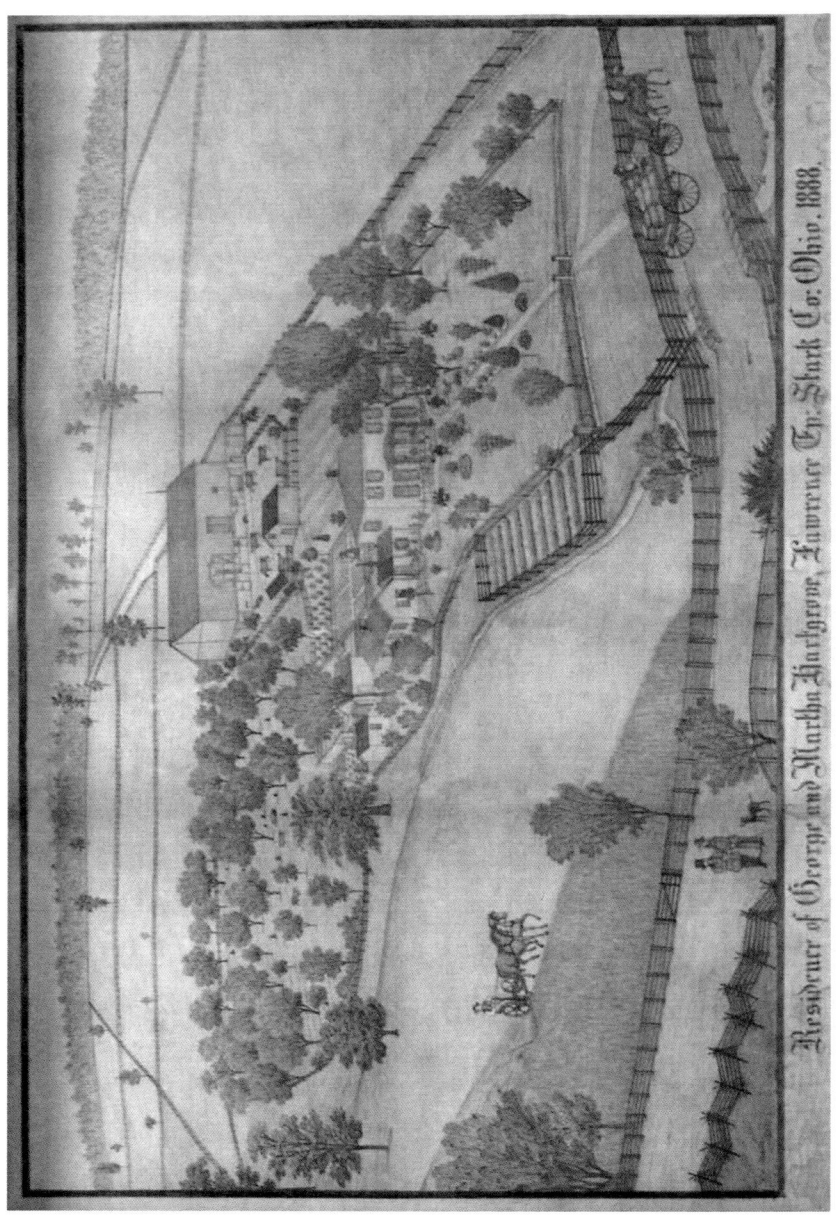

Residence of George and Martha Hardgrove, Lawrence Tp. Stark Co. Ohio. 1888.

FOLK ARTIST FERDINAND BRADER: He lived with George and Martha Hardgrove for months in 1888 while depicting their home and farm on Butterbridge Road (*William McKinley Museum*).

AMERICAN HOUSE HOTEL IN MASSILLON c 1860: Crowds filled Main Street (now Lincolnway) as dynamic speakers addressed them from the balcony (*Massillon Museum*).

MASSILLON, OHIO DEPOT: Civil War soldiers received heartfelt send-offs from here. Later, as word about victories was sent to the telegraph office, the cannon placed by the hill shot 100 rounds to spread the news. *(Massillon Museum).*

O. J. HARDGROVE: Orrick Hardgrove's Ads ran in 1865 editions of Massillon Independent newspapers. It was an era of innovative agricultural machines and tools, and he had several local businessmen interested in buying his patent rights *(Massillon Independent Newspaper)*.

FOREWORD

Through letters sent back and forth to her sons, Margaret Jackson Hardgrove passionately kept track of not only her immediate family but intertwining lives of Hardgrove(s) and neighbors. Those on the home front and those serving in the war.

During the months and years of war, it seemed her carpet bag was always on the move with her frequent travels by stage coach, canal boat and train. And as she spent time with a daughter here or son there, she kept her pen rolling, reporting all the events. As those two items—carpet bag and pen—were her main-stays, it, seemed fitting to use them for part of the title of this collection of letters. Still, the title needed a bit more.

The idea of Cross Keys, symbolized by 3 large, old house keys, reflected an awesome intertwining of lives—each family line represented by a key. The name, Cross Keys, was from a 19th century inn that was in Washington County, Pennsylvania where Margaret and husband John and the various Hardgrove families lived before moving to Ohio. Perfect name for this book portraying three family lines whose paths continued to cross during the Civil War.

But further images of cross keys have evolved in more recent decades, illustrating how the letters have crossed the country several times and finally made it back to Stark County.

After searching for Hardgrove history for nearly 15 years on my own, I was known as the genealogist for our line of the family. That is what prompted cousin Ralph Edward Hardgrove of Canal Fulton to direct another cousin to call on me. His name was Earl Kulgoski. He had spent half his life searching for details on the Hardgrove(s), as well. After we got acquainted, he, then, began sending me bits and pieces of information that might advance my work, and I did the same—again, cross keys.

One day an "Earl packet" arrived, and it was heavier. Inside were dozens of Margaret's letters that had (a quarter-century before) been transcribed and turned over to him by cousin Ruth Hardgrove Finch—again, crossed keys. Ruth was a great-granddaughter of Margaret's and she, too, had spent years trying to piece together the family history and reconnect to the

Hardgrove descendents here in Lawrence Township and Massillon. Since the letters mentioned both Earl's line and my line of the family, he hoped reading them might help my quest in sorting out the relatives and lead us both to further insights.

Over the next several decades of reading and *rereading* portions of the letters—so rich with historical vitality covering Stark County, Wayne County, Tuscarawas County, Holmes County and Southwestern Pennsylvania–I kept thinking, it would be a shame if Margaret's letters and Henry's letters idled, unread, in someone's file cabinet for yet another half century. But neither Earl nor I knew just what to do about that, except to donate them for the shelves of a library at some future time.

The final instance of cross keys came after cousin Earl died, and I inherited all of his research—books, notes, letters, maps. In following up on some very old correspondence in his file, I got in touch with one of my great-grandmother's distant relatives, Helen Strine. Great-grandmother's name was Sabina (Strine) Hardgrove; a name was all I had ever known. Helen soon sent me letters Sabina had written in the aftermath of the Civil War. Sabina's writings offered a whole new perspective.

And so, all these descendants, representing three distinct lines of Hardgrove(s), contributed to unlocking this treasure-trove of Civil War era experiences, from the very beginning of the war to the very end. I look forward to sharing the letters, herein, and stories they contain. I believe cousins Earl and Ruth would be pleased that their contributions to Ohio history will find a place in The William McKinley Presidential Library and Museum, along with some other wonderful Hardgrove artifacts.

Kathryn Hardgrove Popio

PREFACE

In reading these wonderfully-descriptive Civil War letters written by Margaret Jackson Hardgrove and her soldier son, John "Henry" Hardgrove, I was totally focused on *their* experiences—on the home front near Massillon, Ohio and on Henry's regimental sites.

Only gradually did I think about the person who picked up the letters at the post office, took them home, opened the letters and sat down and read them. Who was the elusive "William" or "Willy" as Margaret playfully addressed him on occasion? Who was behind Henry's greeting as he started his letters, "Dear brother"?

Yes! Who were these personalities that Margaret and Henry were so fond of that they diligently and passionately recorded every week's news during the course of the Civil War?

As a widow, Margaret made her home with son William Hardgrove in Jelloway, Ohio, a small community north of Mt. Vernon. It soon becomes obvious that, with carpet bag and pen, Margaret spent more time traversing between busy households of her daughters, Mary Archer and Harriet Bahney, in and near Massillon. The attention, ever-so gradually, shifts to William and wife Judith Ann "Ann." They were truly another center for her life and of Henry's focus in letters.

Civil War buffs may appreciate Henry's outstanding job of pin-pointing regimental locations for William. His insights into the war's leadership and injustices are composed, at times, in vivid story form. The sagas of his regiment's migration through the Southern states contain all the local color of a novel. It is easy to believe that William appreciated Henry's encounters with rebel families and struggles with sesesh ideology.

William and Ann would have read the letters with more ease than readers today—a hundred-fifty years later; William knew the writers and array of characters well. Over time and distance, even in transcribed form, the letters were extremely difficult to navigate. For clarity, I have included information within brackets which better introduce people and businesses Margaret mentioned.

Optional spelling is also frequently enclosed with brackets; although, sticking to colloquial versions used by both Margaret and Henry is extremely appealing. As Margaret flowed from one topic to another without punctuation, I have also supplied just a few more "periods" so readers pause less.

The same kind of care was used when including emotionally-charged letters of Sabina Strine Hardgrove. Custom of the day restrained mention of things that might have helped her write letters which more fully describe circumstances taking place in the aftermath of war. I have included references to historic timeframes about enormous events with their effects trickling down into communities in America, in case some are not used to pondering this period in our country's history. Readers should remember (if one has ever tried their hand at writing), that putting family events down on paper often lacks impact of reality. By including genealogical details, more truth also evolved about what her family back in Pennsylvania was living through.

Finally, I have used tiny footnotes that indicate support for portrayal of people, places and resources throughout the book. While many more might have been employed, I have chosen not to interfere overly-much with the essence of reading letters from real people. I trust that these notes enhance the ability to appreciate them, rather than detract from them.

Trains, Boats and Stage Coaches

The spectacular letters of Margaret Jackson Hardgrove provide a window into the lives of her children, her neighbors, and various communities she frequented during the vital years of 1858 to 1865. With her son's enlistment in the Civil War, Margaret also shared her deep interest in every aspect of its effect. Her letters, back and forth with her son and family members, unfold vivid details and human interest stories of the war and serve to preserve part of Stark County history that would otherwise be lost. She was a natural writer. So much so that it is easy to imagine Margaret being born with pen in hand!

Auburn-haired[1] Margaret Jackson Hardgrove paid no heed to the rushing waters of the Tuscarawas when crossing east by buggy on Butterbridge Road. Trotting horse hooves and rumbling wagon wheels on hard dirt road drowned it out as she and husband John headed toward the Village of Canal Fulton. One sure stop in town would be the post office where letters might be waiting!

John Crawford Hardgrove held his leather reins loosely but raised his voice to be heard as he and Margaret passed Butterbridge farms that were nicely shaping up. They glanced at an occasional property sign like Pleasant Grove and Quiet Home[2] that meant these families were putting down roots instead of heading westward to Indiana, Missouri or Kansas as so many others had. Traveling as a soldier during the War of 1812,[3] John had found Ohio an appealing area. In later years, he eventually returned and brought his family to where cousins already resided.[4]

Margaret, a prolific letter-writer, made sure family news never got cold. She could hardly stand it until she got pen to paper letting folks in Pennsylvania know things like how their son Orrick (O. J.) and wife Rachel were fairing after losing 8-month-old daughter Sarah J.[5] News returning from Washington County would be a treat to find at the post office on Canal Street. They planned to visit back home again, some day. By 1852, folks eagerly awaited the railroad line from Pittsburgh to Massillon and Orrville and Wooster.[6] It was fun to discuss it and think of all the extra places they would stop to see along the way.

Those plans melted, though, when John died in autumn 1852,[7] just as the railroad's arrival was celebrated. Margaret spent the next few years moving from Lawrence Township and handling their affairs. In July of '57, she then helped O. J. cope with Rachel's death[8] and the next year daughter Harriet's wedding. Letters became vital links with her children, passed along with loving concern from one household to another. From those pages, they knew how she was faring as well as activities and state of health of each of her three sons and four daughters.

As a widow, she formally made her home with her son William Hardgrove, a teacher and farmer, north of Mt. Vernon, Ohio.[9] Becoming highly in demand as a house guest during the early 1860's, however, she would visit each child nearly as much as she stayed home. Her daughter and son-in-law, Mary and George Archer, owned a farm on Pigeon Run Road[10] south of Massillon and Canal Fulton, where Margaret's 15-year-old daughter, Minerva, boarded as Margaret traveled. Daughter Harriet and husband Hiram Bahney lived closer to the Village of Massillon.

with their son. No matter where she stayed from one week to the next during the period of 1858 to 1865, everyone was in touch through letters.

As we are introduced to Margaret here in her letters of October 1858, she and son John Henry Hardgrove, age 21, just completed a trip back to Washington County Pennsylvania to see family and friends. Riding the "carrs" [railroad train] was quite a smokey adventure. Though the loud whistle announcing the train's arrival into town was even more of a distraction than the blast of the stage coach horn, most   everyone was proud to have it stop in their town. They were proud and eager to take a trip themselves.

Henry (as she called him) accompanied her as far as Pittsburg, with her venturing south to Washington County for the summer. In early autumn, he returned to Pittsburgh to see the fair and meet up with Margaret to accompany her home. They traveled several hundred miles during summer and early autumn of 1858, not hesitating to avail themselves of every mode of transportation of the time until even Margaret was wore out

"When I get home once more," she wrote to William, "I will try and stay there."

Stay in the tiny village of Jelloway[11] (near Mt. Vernon) when she could be tending to Minerva's guidance, helping Mary with canning or enjoying all the social activities that places like Massillon and Orrville provided? Old friends also invited her to visit for a few days, as had been the case that   summer and early autumn of 1858. She described her Pennsylvania trip like this:

Massillon   Oct. 10th '58   William Hardgrove

Well Willie Here we are again we arrived safe here on Tuesday two

oclock Henry after spending two days at the fair at pittsburg came

up to brownsville on the boat and from that to uniontown on the

coach [stagecoach] found me at James McCleans a fryday. He staid

til monday we went to Conelsville in the coach took diner there got

on the carrs [passenger railroad train] at two oclock arrived at

pittsburg a litle after dark eat our supers went to the theater returned to the Mantion house [Mansion House inn at Borough of Washington, Pennsylvania][12] got to bed slept but litle got up eat breakfast and got aboard the carrs started for home . . ."

Arriving at Massillon, they went directly to see her married daughter, Mary and husband George Archer, a Massillon wagon maker, where daughter Minerva was a frequent boarder. Though Margaret, herself, had a "lame back" and a cold by that time, she found Minerva was already sick with the ague [a malaria-type sickness resulting from the bite of a mosquito]. So she stayed at the Archers for several more weeks until Minerva showed what one might call unusual signs of improvement.

continuing Oct. 10th letter

This morning she has no fever Dr. Jeramia shorter is attending her but she is pevish as a baby she at a bowl of oister soup this morning and I am in hopes she will soon be able to be out of bed. I want to get home and see you . . . I am in hopes I will in about two weeks. they had a good fair some say there were ten or fifteen thousand people thare. Hariet said she saw unkle John Hall thare and Curtis Downs. Hariet says she has began a letter to you she will finish it soon. she has not ben well since she had the first attack of the feever I have a bad cold and had a lame back from traviling in the coach and carrs so I cant tel yet when I wil be home as Minerva gets well or able to be out of bed . . . I have given her about nine or ten doses of quinine since yesterday morning.

She ended her October letter harmoniously reminiscing about her lengthy vacation in Pennsylvania saying, "I have not spent a summer for many years so pleasantly. the friends were all very kind. george paul got his picture taken for me he is a very agreeable man." [George Paull may have been an attorney friend in Washington County where she and her husband once lived.][13]

4

The Civil War began April 1861, but it took time to recruit and organize any kind of official state of war. In every community speeches were made from town centers and church pulpits. Some boys' responses were immediate, others gradual. Will Archer, brother-in-law of Margaret's daughter, Mary, was reported to have joined quickly but had his father upset. "His father was very angry," Margaret wrote, "and said he would fecth him back but he has given it up now."

Massillon   August 27, 1861   William Hardgrove

Dear son will [Archer]wrote to his father from camp chase at columbus. they ware sent to Mansfield and he wrote Minerva from thare. Last wednesday Mary sent charly [possibly Archer's handy man] down with the buggy for me to come and put a quilt in for her I went and put it in the frames that evening the next day Mrs. thomson and mrs. Wilson come up and helpt me. Mary help me some a fryday and saterday I got it out about four oclock a sunday. Minerva came up and I came down to town with her last night . . . the soldiers ware marching up and down the street Minerva and I took a walk down street as far as the bridge [stone canal bridge in Massillon] and we ware both very tired when we got back. we thought we would best Henry coming in . . . but he came up here after we came back he had been at the Fremont Hall at a military meeting. he belongs to a company of home gards though they are liable to be cald in to the service whenever they are needed . . . I got plenty of Buckleburys without the trouble of hunting them among the laurel and rattle snakes. M. Hardgrove
p s I had forgoten to say I am well

Butterbridge Road

Margaret and her family members were settling into a normal flow by 1859. Meanwhile, a second line of Hardgrove(s), those who lived on the Hardgrove homestead on Butterbridge Road in Lawrence Township, were entering a transition of their own. Though none of Margaret's letters were kept from 1859 or 1860, when the letters resumed, she began mentioning "Mitchel." For that reason, an introduction to Mitchell H. Hardgrove would be helpful. It begins briefly near March of 1861 as he is leaving the farm where he grew up. Then, through flashbacks, the circumstances that led up to his departure will be uncovered.

As the endless winter of 1861 seemed to tire of sending frigid weather and snow storms to obscure the farms and roads south of Canal Fulton, Mitchell Hardgrove rode his horse down the wide lane of Uncle George Washington Hardgrove's farm on Butterbridge Road. He was finally firm in his decision to leave there, for the second time.

The first time he left was when he was 19. Leaving the Hardgrove homestead, then, was just a matter of good sense. Having been raised there,[14] he had become a part of the extended family of farmers. Uncle George, with whom he lived, owned the south half of the original farm after Mitch's grandmother Rose died.[15] Uncle John M. Hardgrove and bachelor uncle, William Martin Hardgrove, owned the north half.

Uncle Will was hardly older than Mitch but had bought in as a partner with Uncle John early-on. He, like his older brothers, was dedicated to farm life. They looked forward to making their farms prosperous and raising families right there where their father Richard Hardgrove, one of the first two Constables of Lawrence Township, had settled in 1812.[16] Not Mitch, though.

He never aspired to become a farmer, though he had already helped shear sheep, clean stalls, bale hay, cut wheat and plant plenty of rye on his uncles' farms.[17] In these changing times, new businesses were being established in the burgeoned town of Massillon. Having also chopped his share of trees to build fences on the farm, a saw mill presented the first likely employment. After all, the railroad had just recently come all the way through from Pittsburgh to Massillon to Orrville and Wooster. Lumber for ties was an important commodity[18] in plans for expansion across Ohio, Indiana and on to Chicago. Jobs for supplying the demand were plentiful.

Whereas, in former decades, adventures were sought in clearing forests to create farmable land, building cabins and expanding the Ohio-Erie canal all the way to the Ohio River, those times belonged to previous generations. He had heard dozens of stories his father Robert and Aunt Ruth (Hardgrove) Earl[19] told of "back in the day . . ." Now he and his cousins Henry and George Earl were eager to carve out futures of their own. Unlimited opportunities were out there if a young man was willing to work hard and save his money.

Where he boarded for a while, there was always someone sharing Canton newspaper ads and scuttebutt about buying land out West. One could make the decision to buy ahead of time or take a chance and see what was really out there before making a purchase.

In fact, Aunt Mary Hardgrove was the first to leave the farm and do just that. Not long after marrying William Shaefer in March of 1845, they went West to Indiana.[20] Their daughter Rose was born out there.[21] But

Uncle Shaefer took sick and died after just a couple of years, so she returned to the farm before getting her own place. Mitch's cousin O. J. already owned land—site unseen—in Kansas. Mitch enjoyed the talk of going West, and even sat with the fellas imagining which state they might choose had they the notion to aim for that. But Massillon was as far as he intended to go right then, himself, since meeting Hannah Justus.

In those early years of boarding in town, he met all kinds of new people, including Hannah's older brother William Justus. He was also a miller and lived in town. When Mitch met William's 17-year-old sister, no two ways about it, he was smitten.

After courting and getting to know each other, they decided to get married. He was 21, the required age for a man to apply for a marriage license, and Hannah was 18. They were married by their minister on February 23, 1860.[22]

Though Mitch worked at the mill, he also occasionally returned to help his uncles. But he and Hannah enjoyed living closer to downtown and her parents and close to Mitch's aunt and uncle, Ruth and Gilberthorp Earl. They could also ride over to see the Archers, where Hannah and Minerva always enjoyed chatting.

During the first year of establishing their home, the newspaper was full of increasingly-tense articles of potential war. When they were invited to Sunday dinner, no matter at whose house it was, plenty of opinions were offered about what the country should do to resolve red-hot issues. But the couple's own conversations, long about summer, were centered on discovery that Hannah was expecting a child. It would be born around Christmas.

On the fourth day of the New Year of 1861, their baby arrived. It was a boy.[23] They named him Willy, as William was a favorite name on both sides of the family.

Instead of regaining strength after the birth confinement, however, there were complications. Hannah died a week later, on January 11, 1861.[24]

With time off from the mill, Mitch left Willy in the care of Hannah's parents and returned to board on Butterbridge for a while. Each week as he rode his horse into Massillon to visit Willy, preparation for war was gaining momentum in town.

Should he stay to work for Uncle George? Go back to the mill? Should he go West? (No, that was also getting more problematic.) What about Willy? And just how would losing men to the war affect jobs right there in Massillon and Canton? They needed men to keep the mills running steadily, which would also keep the farmers producing.

As the winter let up in 1861, he went out on Sundays to ride around the fields and woods, debating. So many thoughts swirled in his mind, as he tried to remember each and every precious conversation with Hannah. So little of it prepared him for now, though.

Uncle George and Aunt Martha offered him room to stay. Should he? The first time he left the farm, he was positive leaving was right. What would Hannah want for Willy? She so looked forward to bringing up the baby in Massillon near her family. So that was the answer.

This time as his horse left tracks in the muddy lane and fields and along Butterbridge, thoughts of Hannah returned to help him bid goodbye to the homestead. He and Willy could always visit now and then. They wouldn't be that far away, after all

Massillon

August 27, 1861

Wm. Hardgrove

Dear son I received your letter and went to Mrs. Doxeys and she is willing to take lucinda [Lucinda is Willliam's 9-year-old niece] as soon as you can bring her the union school commenced yesterday and if she had been here she could have started in at the first of the school I think Ann [probably Margaret's daughter near Mt. Vernon, Ohio] had beter see to her clothes have her some good under cloths and nough of dresses and aprons . . . the fair here will be the 25 26 27 or28 of sept.

Michel Hardgrove is working for george archer he is learning the trade he has been boarding with them til this week last saturday week michel and Henry [John Henry] went to orrville. Mich has a horse here at archers and they hired a horse of Mr. Cotton and put two horses in the buggy and that night cottons horse

9

got sick they had two veterenary horse doctors in attendance but the horse died they had him opened and his heart and lungs were so much diseased that it was impossible for him to lived any longer Henry paid the Doctor bills and funeral expenses and I dont think Mr. Cotton can recover any things more Minerva was up to fulton on a visit she was gone nearly two weeks . . . doc Houts got his leg broke and they have taken him to cleaveland to have it taken off just below the calf of his leg

Hariet has got her photagraph pictures they are the best pictures I ever saw of her. Henry got one of them last night. Hariet says she wanted you to bring her some red paper if we have any at home and I wish you would bring me a pair of woolen stockings and a canton flanel jacket with sleeves for I dont expect to go home til some time in october. tomorrow there is to be a big animal show here and probably we will al go to see it Mary says she wants to go and take her children Henry has settled with Mr Cotton had nothing to pay but the hire of the horse and Doctor bill and funeral expenses I was veery sorry to hear that constance [William's infant daughter] was unwell litle Delia [Mary's infant daughter]²⁵ was very sick last week but she is better now write by next monday mail and say when you will bring lucinda in give my best regard to Dr. Most and family my love to all the dear young folks at home
your Mother M. Hardgrove
p s I had forgoten to say I am well

Massillon Ohio

Oct. 6, '61

Mr. Wm. Hardgrove

Dear brother: having enlisted in the Glorious Cause of our County, I embrace the earliest oportunity of writing to you. I put my name down last thursday. yesterday afternoon I was sworn in and mustered into service.

Mr. Briggs a turner in our shop is the man that is getting up the company.

He is a Christian and a scholar, but not a good judge of whiskey.

Tomorrow morning I am to receive my papers and start out recruiting I am going to help raise the company and I will give them the best turn in the shop for second lueutenant. Eighteen have enlisted. It is going to take us some time to raise our Company. I think we will do well if we raise it in two months. I want to come out and see you if I can before I go.

Mother is at our house and well as comon.

Our fair this year was a poor thing it lasted six days. I was over at the Canton fair last friday it was very good. There was the largest crowd of people there that I ever saw at a county fair. I cant write much this time. write and let me know if you think there is any show for volinteers out there. If you think it best I will send some bills and have a meeting at your school house [Jelloway, Ohio, near Mt. Vernon] and try the boys that way. Let me hear from you soon. Your brother J. H. Hardgrove

In Memorial
of
Willy Hardgrove[26]

Born January 4, 1861
Died October 11, 1861

Son of
Mitchell H. and Hannah (Justus) Hardgrove

Massillon Ohio

Oct. 22nd '61

Mr. Wm. Hardgrove

Dear brother, I thought I would write you a few lines this morning and let you know how we are getting along.

We have 64 men enrolled and 57 or them sworn in. Mitchel Hardgrove has enlisted and George Earl. I have been trying to get old rusty Park Hardgrove to enlist but all in vain he is bound to loaf around off his poor relations not able to take care of themselves.

I will be at your house next week some time and I would like to bring 3 or 4 good fellow along home with me. Orrick is working for George [Archer] at the wagons.

Harriet is not very well. Mother will go home till after our company leaves. Nothing more at present.

I remain your brother

J. H. Hardgrove

Camp Medill

Henry and members of his Company left Massillon's depot with carpet bags in hand and headed south through Ohio to Camp Medill for training. In this chapter, he also put pen to paper and wrote home about the men's adventurous ride on the carrs, meals of "fat pork boild," getting uniforms, poor leadership, and lack of pay. At spring's end, he eventually got into heavy issues of camp life and their approach to Corinth. Meanwhile, Margaret's pen flies to record happenings in the Archer's and Bahney's households and the Canal Fulton community's response to the war.

Lancaster, Ohio
No. 11th '61
Mr. Wm. Hardgrove

Dear brother I received your letter the day before we left but not in time to answer it before we left. We started from Massillon a friday morning at seven oclock There was a very large crowd to see us off.

Tears flowed freely in every direction. We all left Merrily and gay, at lest a good man let on so.

We went to Mansfield and there changed carrs. It is a very beautiful county from Mt. Vernon to Newark The corn looked well.

Close to Newark I saw the white Cassimere goats. they white as snow and about 15 or 20 of them The wool is very long. We changed carrs at Newark and went Zanesville It was about sundown when we left Newark but what I could see of the way side it was very mountainous and rockey. We got into Zanesville about eight oclock.

We marched out carpet sack and blanket in hand we formed into double file and stood in the street for about one hour and a half while the captain went up street and found loging for us, he came back and marched us up to the city Odd fellow hall a very commodious and well furshed hall.

After staying there about one hour longer the quartermaster of the regiment forming there prepared super for us; we were marched up to the other hall and took supper which was mighty poor. We had some fat pork boild, rye slop to drink bread and butter. From there we marched back to the hall and prepared for bed…which consisted of

15

two benches faced together, we laid on blanket on blanket on the benches and throwed the other one over us Phil Tillton and bunked together. Toward morning I got cold, I put on my overcoat and laid down and slept till morning.

In the morning I went to the market house which was full and plenty. About eight oclock in the morning we had an other breakfast like the supper; then we marched down to the depot broke rank and took a trip through the town as we had to stay there till eleven oclock. I visited the glass works, which was very interesting to me as I had never seen anything of the kind before. I then took a look at the railroad bridge that crosses the Muskingham river; it was the most splendit thing of the kind that I ever saw. It is about two hundred yards long. The most of the material used in its construction is iron, which is used in abundance. There is a foot path on one side just above the bridge is a large dam. The water pooring over looks splended.

There are some very fine buildings in the place The road from Zanesville to this place passes through a very mountainous country. this side of Zanesville we passed through a tunnel about a quarter of a mile long; it was perfectly dark while passing through I could not see the fellow that was sitting a long side of me.

We got into this place abut two oclock saterday afternoon. The regimental bands were present and a few of the citizens and escorted us to our barricks. Our baricks is a large brick building about 400 feet long and 75 feet wide. It was used for a starch factory; and broke

16

down. Our bunks are large enough for six to sleep in there are three in a teer one above the other. I had the good luck to get the top burth. I dont think much of four regimental officers. They may deceive their looks. I have been appointed surgent by the colonel until officers are elected.

We did not get anything to eat on saturday till after night and then it was every fellow for himself and got all they wanted while others got nothing; we have a little more system about it now. We get fresh beef and beans and potatoes coffee with sugar in it bread but no butter. We have four or five fellows to cook for us. On sunday morning we received some uniforms. We got the womis shirt, pants drawers, cap, socks and blanket. the blankets are very good. After we got our uniforms the Major took us to the M.E. church and heard a very good sermon.

If you have not sent that blanket you need not now. I have two good ones and Tilton has two so we can sleep very comfortably.

Write soon. Direct. J. H. Hardgrove

Camp Medill   Care of Colonel Schleich Camp

Lancaster, O.
Jan. 6th '62
Mr. Wm. Hardgrove
Dear brother I received your letter a few minits ago containing $20

It cam in mighty good play. I borrowed two dollars of a fellow some time ago and it has simmered down to less than a postage stamp.

17

I would have had plenty of money if I had not lent any.

Our fellows wanted to go home and had no money. I lent them all the money I had and borrowed more for them with the promise of them paying it when they came back. but nary red have I seen since they come back harder up than when they left

The most of them were married men and some of their family sick. So as long as I had a red I could not refuse them.

There are so many of our officers absent that I can not go home for a week or ten days. Lieut. Blackburn is at home and three of our sergeants and three corporals. So I will have to wait until they come back.

I have more to see to than any of the other officers. I have to attend the drilling every day and see that it goes off right. Our company is far the best drilled company in camp. They come up to the work like regulars. Our company is the only one noticed in town. Tell mother I will send her my picture that she requested.

When I go home I will stop at Mt. Vernon and go by the way your house.

I will only get to go home once till the war is over so will have to divide my time.

We have good sleighing here now.

I will write to you before I start.

Write soon and let me know how the children are.

Your brother   Lieut. J. H. Hardgrove

Camp Medill
Lancaster O.
Jan. 20 '62
Mr. Wm. Hardgrove
Dear brother

Under present circumstances I will leave for home or
Massillon this afternoon. I am going with the Captains wife or I would
go by the way of your home.

We received orders yesterday to hold ourselves in rediness to
leave at any time. As I return from Massillon I will stop at hour house,
which will be the last of this week or the first of next. I will write to you
again from Massillon.

> *Yours in haste*
> *your brother*
> *Lieut. J. H. Hardgrove*

Massillon   *March 12, 1862*
Mr. William Hardgrove
Dear son I arrived here safe about a quarter before seven that evening
had my baggage put in the buss and rode up to Hariets I found Hariet
sick in bed she had been very sick for two weeks but she is better now
she had inflamation in the stomach Mary said she was very bad at the
time she wrote but she did not want to let me know it for I might feel
worried or alarmed and the weather was so bad maybe I could not
come in. Delia Hay [boarder and/or relative] is at Hariets again she
come last monday she says charley [possibly Delia's husband] has

19

gone to old philadephia yesterday. Mary sent charley [possibly driver at Archer's carriage shop] for me. Mary is not very well she has been taking blue pills for the liver disease though she is fleshyer than she has been for ten years. I give Henry his mony last night [possibly 1Henry Archer, George's brother] and this morning he paid it over to george [Archer]. they say orrich and Henry [Archer] both thinks of geting Maried. O J is in for shorlot sterling I dont know the girls name that Henry is after. little Delia [Mary Archer's 2 year-old daughter] had a bad cough and sore throat she coughed last night all night they have plenty of aples here they have had fresh fish have oysters evy few days fryd oysters and oyster soup they have four fresh milch cows and make lots of butter they say it is 18 cents per pound Minerva sells a good deal of buter. Mary Mae [neighbor or friend] is here at Archers her and Minerva are cuting up two very fat chickens on the table here whare I am writing It has been snowing all day nearly thare has two large droves of milch cows went by her a few days ago and staid all night about a mile from here and one of the cows had a fine large calf with two heads as compleet as any other calf both head grew out of the one neck. george [Mary's husband] has just hired a boy to work here on the farm. he has philip in the shop [carriage shop]. old brother John whitacker and george [Archer] and Henry [possibly George's brother] have been surveying the Road today but it is so mudy they did not finish. I expect he will here tomorrow . . . they [Minerva and Mary

Mae] are talking so that I write over two or threee times. george and Henry have come home write soon your Mother
M Hardgrove

[John Henry's letter home without greeting, probably April, 1862]
Being exposed so much during the engagement on the 6 & 7 of April and afterwards that I caught a very bad cold. I felt worse than I have since I have been in the service. I am all right again and appetite as good as ever

We have a very good regiment and all we want is some one for a leader Our Col is Commander of the brigade that we are in the Lieut. Col. his brother is a poor excuse. When we get into a fight he is always drunk. And he dont know enough about tactics to lead a regiment when he is sober.

The doctors are not worth a snap. They are from Newark and the Newark men are all they will pay any attention to. Seven of the companie are from Newark and surounding hill country. the other three companies. Two are from Stark and one from Columbiana County.

The Newark companies are the favored ones at Head Quarters. The Lieut. Col. and Major are sick so the Captains of Cos. A. & B have charge of the regiment.

The Captain of Co. B is sick. We are the third ranking company in the regiment which is company C although we are acting as company I. On account of the Captain of the Co. B being sick Cap. Briggs should be Lieut. Col. which position is given to a Newark Captain.

Our adjitant has resigned and they are going to appoint a Sergeant out of a Newark Company in his place. If they do their will be a big fuss in Camp and their will be before long anyhow. Unless we are treated better at Head Quarters and our rights respected you should not be surprised to hear of the commissioned officers of Co. I. 76 reg. O.V. resigning. Nine days more and we will be in the service seven months without any pay. When we first came into the regiment They told us we were luckey for getting into their regiment that it was the Pet regiment of the state. It looks like it now. Other regiments have been paid off that have not been in the service. I do not want to resign while we are expecting a big fight evry day but as soon as it is over if we are not paid off there will be a good many commissioned officers resign. I would rather be under col. Schleich of the 61st than any Col. I know of.

He is a man that has some respect for the officers under him. He is a talented man. An officer that can take his men into a fight and take them out again. We have got some mighty good fighting men and all they want is a good leader and they will make their mark. The Old

Col. is a good officer. He maneuvred us throughout the fight here in a good order.

He has command of the Brigade now and will not be with us.

He is the man that Commanded the State of the West when she went to reinforce Fort Sumter.   *[No signature]*

Massillon   *April 30th*   *(1862)*

Dear son [William] according to promise I take the pen to give you a skech of the passing events of the last four days when we arrived at orrville O J was not thare but my old friend Wily come and carried our bagage up to the hotel [The Hurd House]27 and went to hunt O J which he did in a few minits we ware very comfortably entertained stopd thare til ten oclock next day saw Brother Harison. James (Jones) had a talk with him had a call from Dr. Ade Miller [A. C. Miller]28 the next morning called at his house in company with O J and Minerva. Orrich got our tickets come with us to Massillonq put us and our carpet sacks in the bus and he went on to canton [Canton, Ohio] came back that night he sold forty achers of land in Mo [Missouri] that morning at orrville to son of cease. the first person I saw at Hiram Bahneys was Selina she has been thare a week [boarding] talks of going to holms [Holmes County] for want of spase. I must be brief on some subjects but will give you the particulars on my return. Henry [possibly Henry Archer, Mary's brother-in-law] came down a sunday with the buggy for me. orrich come up to georges [Archer] a sunday staid til monday. Henry and george says they are going with me home [Mt. Vernon] and O J said he would go too they say in three weeks two from next saterday. the excitement of the war has somewhat subsided the people here and every whare have been allmost mad with the excitement a preacher in carrall fulton [Canal Fulton] two weeks ago went to church to preach to his congregation he commenced with the present state of the publick feelings and soon got so excited that he calld on all the young men present to go and offer their thare service to fight the enemy and they should rise to thare feet all that ware willing to go when twelve or 15 young men rose they ware waggons got ready and they all went to canton the same day an sunday offered Capt Sam Beath thare services and are waiting to go when calld on. the citizens of Massillon will not tolerate tory talk. old David atwater is treatend well Mary sent down for Hariet today she has just come we have a fat chicken for dinner with a great variety of condiments and extras when I come to orrville I was told that Henry [different Henry] had gone with the Massillon company but he was not gone though he had offered his service I left the room when Hariet come and miss Delia [Mary's little girl] come in and you see what she has done to my letter scrachd and daubd it all up Mary has tomato plants and cucumber large enough to set out I have had several meses of dandaline salet I will write next week or the week after write soon Henry will send you some paper

your Mother   M Hardgrove

Camp Lieut. Wallace Tenn.
May 11, 62
Mrs. M A Archer
Dear sister I received your letter day before yesterday of the 26 int.

It was the first one that I receive from home since the Fight. I had almost come to the conclusion you was not going to write.

It is one week today since we came to this camp but it is a different day from what it was last sunday. We left camp Shilch about two o'clock in a hard rain. It rained all afternoon as hard as I ever saw it rain. I had a good gum cloak that kept me dry. We marched 6 miles and night came on and we encamped here where we have been ever since and expect to remain till we go away which will be soon. We are under marching orders subject to leave at half an hour notice. Yesterday we fell into line of battle for to leave stood there till dark and then received orders to go back to camp.

We had a very hard time of it the afternoon and night we came here. It rained all night. Our team stalled with our tents and baggage two miles back. In the morning our Company had to go on picket for twenty four hours. About noon the sun came out and the boys dried out their wet clothes and were all right again. We have got a poop place to camp. It is on the side of a hill in the woods as usual.

Our division (Wallace) is kept back as a reserve. Our regiment now instead of being the advance is the rear regiment. The advance regiments are within four miles of Corinth. They are having some heavy skirmishing there. Night before last Gen. Pope made an attack on the rebels and lost 200 men killed wounded and prisoners.

It is the general impression among the officers that we wont have much of a fight at Corinth.

Prisoners that come in lately day they are evacuating. It is my impression we will have a fight with them here before they leave. Next week we will have possession of Corinth and the Rebels will either have to fight or run.

One of our men died a few days ago by the name of McClure with the Diarrhea He lived in Massillon and is a married man with a large family of small children. He was a very good soldier and a useful man in our Company. He was a good painter. There is a young fellow by the name of Ott very sick and not expected to live. I do not know what ails him. It is some kind of billious disease. Nine tenths of the disease is of a billious nature. There was upwards of twenty reported on the sick list this morning to the Sergeion [surgeon].

We have about two hundred thousand soldiers her and not more than one hundred twenty thousand of them are fit for duty.

Mitch Hardgrove is well and driving team Geo. Earl [another cousin] is well. I thought Henry Hardgrove [another line of Hardgrove(s)] was in the 64 regiment . . . His reg is in the advance about twelve miles from here now . . . We are now fifteen miles from Corinth. Everything is very forward here. the wheat has been out in head for a long time. But it . . . [letter abruptly halted thoughts here].

The Captain is waiting on me to go with him to get some cherry bark to make bitters with and I must close.

Your brother   Lieut. J. H. Hardgrove

Direct to Tittsburg Landing
Tennessee river Tenn.

Mother wanted to know what the impression was here about the closing of the war. It is generally believed that we will be at home till the 4th of July.

We get the daily papers here now.
May 15th
Since I wrote the above we changed camps.
We are now four miles closer to Corinth. We have a very poor place camp no water within a mile.

We have heard very heavy canonading yesterday afternoon.
Last night we had a heavy thunderstorm It rained very hard

Your brother, Lieut. J. H. Hardgrove

All Talk and No Money

Margaret's letters in late Spring of 1862 created a paper collage of events. After savoring John Henry's news, she once again picked up her pen to pass along his details to her other son in Mt. Vernon, Ohio. Interspersed with descriptions of the "boys" increasing discontent with leadership in their regiment were snippets of Lawrence Township events and sketches of local personalities. Among them "Hamilton" will be noted several times, bringing the third line of Hardgrove(s) into the scope of her observations. *At this point*, however, Hamilton Hardgrove (and wife Sabina) will be only briefly introduced. Then in a much later chapter Sabina's own personal letters will contribute yet another Civil War era portrait, quite different from that of cousins—Margaret and the Butterbridge families.

(Introduction for 3rd line of Hardgrove(s): As newlyweds in Fall of 1853, Hamilton and Sabina Hardgrove began boarding with Charles Eckert and wife Ellen on the south edge of the village of Canal Fulton.[29]

Charles was a native of Wurttemburg. Since Sabina came from Pennsylvania-German heritage, the couple had things in common beyond speaking German. The Eckerts had 2 children, David and Adaline, and eventually Hamilton and Sabina also had a child, Eleanor Jane.

Living in close proximity with the Eckerts turned out to be fortunate. At the time that Sabina was expecting the birth of their second child in 1857, all were surprised to hear there was not just one baby but twins. Unfortunately, one twin daughter died.[30] It was a great sadness in their household, but the other girl named Emila [Emily] survived.

When presidential debates began in Illinois in 1858, with the 6-year-old Republican Party participating, the birth of Sabina's and Hamilton's son, Marshall, was a small part of the news that passed from household to household. Most were much more eager for predictions about how candidates of the 4 political parties would square-off. One candidate of the new party was Abraham Lincoln. It took time for information from debates to spread from big city coverage to the average person in Ohio. Meanwhile, local political opinions ran hot on grapevines. Who was Lincoln? Where did he stand? With North or South?

It was an exciting time when the "dark-horse" Republican, Abraham Lincoln, won the election of 1860. But confusion on issues only escalated. For the busy Hardgrove and Eckert households, it was a time of awaiting yet another baby. But in Stark County, at the time, many children were suddenly dying. Sabina (having already lost a child) became overly nervous whenever one of her children or the Eckert's children were ill.

As President Lincoln took office in February 1861, the storm cloud of secession hovered incessantly above the nation. Like awaiting a storm. War? Or no war? Sabina and Hamilton welcomed daughter Rose to their family later that spring. Being parents with 4 little children to raise, Hamilton did not enlist while the men in Lawrence Township were eventually being recruited,

Other worries mixed with concerns of war. If the new president could not help resolve conflicts peacefully, those who stayed on the home front could not count on what the next year might mean to families or businesses. All Hamilton could do was try to get as much employment as he could, working on local farms and doing a little carpentry work to try to get ahead. But it seemed that they were never ahead.

(Note: As Margaret's letters continued, they gradually disclosed this truth.)

Massillon Ohio   May 10th 62   Mr. Wm. Hardgrove

Dear son I arived here safe found them all well I staid at Hirams til after diner the next day and Hariet came with me up to Archers a thursdy evening. thare was a freight train ran off the track on the west side of the river a few rods from the river bridge and broke the engine all to smash I believe thare was only one man hurt. they ran over a cow the track was torn up so they had to work all night. they had received a letter from Henry dated the 26th of April he said they had not received any pay yet and some of the officers had resigned and if they ware not paid off soon more of them would resign. Marshal Blackburn had his resignation wrote and ready to hand in on monday Henry says their col. has comand of a brigad and his brother bill wood has command of thare reg. and he is drunk nearly all the time. he says he dont like to resignd just before a fight but to go in to a big fight with one of the poorest capt. or a drunken col. to lead them they dont like. the last paper says the rebels have not left corinth. the boys are all down on brigggs. henry says he gets sick of his bragodotia. Henry says it was all him and blackburn could do to keep the boys from geting up a petition to have Capt briggs resign. he says the old gal [Mrs. Briggs] keeps him posted as to what the boys writes home about him [Briggs]. Mary says Barbary Meguinn is dead. old peter and polly are living with Julie An [Ann] kirk Beney Hardgrove is living in Massillon and Hamilton is as poor as a dog he has run through all he wound [won] land and all. orrick told me to tell you that he put the tire on one hundred and forty waggon wheels in a day with John Hardgrove [John M. of Butterbridge homestead] to help him. Henry [John Henry] says Michel is driving team and gets 20 dollars per month

I have not saw Minerva yet Hariet said she was coming to her house today. george Archers Mechanical genius is going to be very proffitable to him he says he has got a patent right for iron howns or metal howns for waggons

Doxey has offered him the whold amount of what george was going to give him for this property for his right but Doxey told him he could make more out of it and he had beter keep it. Rusels [The Russels and Co. of Massillon] sent a few waggons out west made with iron howns and now they are in great demand. they would pay Doxey for his property what george was to give for it for his paten right two thousand dollars but they think it will be worth more than that to george.

this is a beautiful pleasant place [daughter Harriet's home] the house is large and thare is two large rooms on the lower story three bedrooms beside a large kitchen two bedrooms up stairs and two large rooms they have the parlor furnished in good stile all new furniture a splendid carpit thirty dollar sopha a set of twenty dollar chairs one rocking chair 20 dollars a bookcase or secratary thirty dollars a center table $20 a what not or corner stand five dollars the center table has an Atlas on it for which george paid 12 dollars.

george wants Henry [John Henry] to come back this is in hopes he will resign and come home but Henry will not doo that til that big fight is over which they expected would come off in ten days from the time he wrote the 26th of April. and if they dont pay them then if he is living he will come home. he dont like the way his regiment has been treated they told him he was luckey to get in that reg. it was the pet reg of the state he says if that is the pet reg of the state he dont want to be in the pet reg. they started on the march with some old worn out mules and waggons they got at fort donalson from the sesesh. no ambulance to carry thair sick or wounded oh I will have to quit and tell you the rest the next time I could write two or three such sheets as this but I have a letter to finish I was writing to Henry

your Mother   M Hardgrove

Camp Lieut. Wallace
Near Monteray Tenn
May 18 '62
Mr. William Hardgrove

Dear Brother

I received your letter and mothers a few day ago of the 26. I commenced answering it but did not feel well enough to finish it.

I have had a light touch of the Yellow jeanders a disease very common here. It does not get a person down in bead all the time but makes him feel mean. I have an appetite to eat but after I done eating half an hour it makes me sick. In a few days I will be all right.

Our Division is the 1st Division of the reserve. Our forces are gradualy closing on Corinth. The most of our advance lines are within four miles of the place. Our advance forces have been skirmishing very heavy for some days back. Yesterday we could hear the roar of the canon nearly all day.

They have been fighting about a large spring which appears to be of a good deal of importance to the Rebels. It is thought by many that the fighting will begin tomorrow (Monday.) If it begins at all I hope it will for I am getting very tired of living in the Wooden Country where all we can see is woods and soldiers.

Our company is becoming very much discouraged and it is hard work to keep them from stacking arms. We have been in the service most eight months and nary read. They still talk about paying us but it is all talk and no money. After this fight is over and we are not paid I will resign. I want to get out of this infernal regiment as soon as possible. If we could have remained in the Old 61st I would never have thought of going home till the war is over.

There is no friendship existing between our company and Head Quarters. We are might independent with them. they dont make mine times off of us

Your Brother Lieut. J. H. Hardgrove

Massillon May 18th 1862 Mrs. J. A. Hardgrove [William's wife]
Dear Ann having pen ink and paper let us try who can write most
and fastest you or I. though I wrote last week I think I must write a
few lines this blessed sabeth day. Hiram and Hariet has not moved in
to thare new house yet it has not been cleaned yet and litle george
has been very sick for three or four days. Dr. Borick was in to see
him this morning he has a very hight fever I think it is scarlet rash.
Henry Heldenbrans little girl died yesterday she will be buried
tomorrow and thare babe is very sick and thare little boy. in truth I
believe all thare children are sick and they have four. the one that
died was next to the oldest she was five or six years old. I received
your letter last thursday with Henrys inclosed. george Archer got a
letter from Henry last monday dated the third of this month. they
ware then a few miles from corinth and have scrimishes with the
rebels nearly every day Mary sent Henry one dollar in a letter I
wrote to him last week. thare was a telegraph dispach came last
week that our troops had taken richmond and they took the canon
down to the Hill on this side of the [Massillon] depot and fired about
a hundred times. a few days after thare came another dispach
confirming it but I believe it was all a hoax. at last lewis Reed son of
Jacob Reed of bridgeport came home from pittsburg landing
wounded in the shoulder he died last week he went to school to
William [Margaret's son now living in Mt. Vernon] when he taught
school [in Lawrence Township]. I saw Ruth oricks Ruth [O. J.'s

34

young daughter]. she was here yesterday morning who says Betsy and Mary [Mitchel's aunts] is going out to Indiana this summer to see Mary's land. Mary is going to take her two children [Rose and George] along to see thare farm [where Mary previously homesteaded]. Cole and Dick [O. J.'s son whom Mary Shaefer cared for since his mother, Rachel, died] will have to board out among the friends till they came back. I believe I forgot to tell you what the disease was that Heldenbrans children had it is inflamation of the lungs and scarlet rash. the folks are going home from church I think thare has been not less than two hundred passd by here since I began to write. some thousand dollar worth of silks cotten and broadcloth. minerva was to come home to Hariets yesterday but owning to sickness and death in the family she cant come till after the funeral. I have written four or five letters since I have been here if anything ocurs here worth writing I will write soon again and I want you to doo so too. tell constance I will fech her the doll when I come home your Mother

M Hardgrove

[Henry's May 23 letter was sent to his sister Mary Archer]
I received two of your letters at the same time. One with newspapers in. If you want to send me papers they will come through the same as letters. I have received all the papers that has been sent to me. Some of our boys receive their papers regular every week from

home. I must stop and take a dish of baked beans and pork and some fresh light bread which all the looks mighty nice.

Well I have had the baked beans and meat and it was mighty good. Soldiering we start out on a march we have generly pritty rust time.

Our bead. We have four forks drove in the ground and two poles across the leaves. On top of the brush are Tenn. [Tennessee] feathers as we call them here. we spread three or four blankets and on top of the blanket we pitch in. Father Briggs sleeps on the front side. Blackburn in the middle and I in the rear.

So the blankets are rather narrow for three. the Captain and I have a fight all night for the best of the blankets.

The Captain and Marsh went out into the country yesterday and got us some very good poam peach pie and buttermilk. I tell you it makes heavy living. I weigh more now than I ever did and feel better. Mitch is sitting on the bead trying to write a letter, Geo. Earl is well. The rest of the company are on picket and I am officer of the guard in Camp.

Tell Het [sister Harriet?] the band is playing "Shells of the Ocean" which sounds mighty nice. Tell her I will be at home in time to take the ip [unclear] in the orchards.

The prospect is good for us to have a little fight tomorrow at Corinth.

This is the best place in the world to try a mans pluck. We have 7 or 8 fellows as big cowards as I ever saw whenever we receive marching orders and they think . . .
[writing ended here]

Massillon   May 25 '62   Mr. Wm. Hardgrove
Dear son I have just returned from the funeral of old Mrs. Hershey [close, former Lawrence Township neighbor]. Mary [Margaret's daughter] and I went up but thare was so many people thare we did not get in the house they had two preachers one spoke Dutch and the other english they had two good long sermons. I saw more of my old aquaintance thare than I would have seen in seven years had I not have been thare. all the Hargroves from Dan to Basheba ware thare and John Linn. Mary and me went round to the back kitchen porch and we got a seat on the porch. betsey Hardgrove and Mary Shaefer [Mitchel's Butterbridge aunts] and Mary elen [wife of Uncle John Hardgrove] and others ware cooking in the wash house. Hamilton Hardgrove was thare he looks poor and lean in flesh. I saw beck kirts or kirk. I think old Mr Hershey will not be long behind the old woman he looks very frail. surely I had the good will of all my old neighbors for every one I met invited me and insisted on me to come

and see them and stay a week and they would convey me round. if I could go to see every one that gave me an invitation today and stay as long as they asked me to stay I would not get home till fall. it was quite refreshing to see so many familiar faces and to have so many friendly greetings. one of the furnaces has started in blast again. Almira [Mary Archer's step-daughter] got a letter from Will [probably brother of George Archer who recently enlisted in war]. he was in the last battle in western virginia. thare was upward of fifty killd and some two or three hundred wounded. Will said they fought the whold afternoon against nearly double thare number and had to fall back to the main body and leave all thare new sibly tents to the rebels as they run out of amunition. the rebels persued them but they got safe to franklin and they ware going to have another fight that day or rather ware at it when he wrote. the boys that had returned to franklin ware left thare to rest and another division went on to meet the army. I got a letters from Henry for minerva out of the office [post office] and she met me at the steps just as I got to Hariets so I dod not get to open it. she done that herself but thare was no news more than what we had it was dated the 19th of this month. thare has been some frost two or three nights past but it don not doo much injury. Rachel stotler lives in Mrs. Dodds house. ephrim Byers works at the coal band tends the ingine. he keeps his Mother. Rachel got in the buggy with Mary and me and invited us on to stop and take diner with her. she had a very good diner and she had the horse waterd and fed. she lives just across the road from Rosey Clapers (alias moris) Roseys husband is in the same reg. that William Archer is in and one or two of his brothers are in the reg that Henry is in Briggs Company. Betsey [Mitch's aunt] says Michel does not write them at all he has not writen since the fight at ft Donelson. all they hear of him is through other boys letters. Benet Hardgrove lives in Massillon his wife apears to be a very agreable woman. Hariet often goes thare. Mary and my self was thare one evening. Mary got a new Brosha shawl. george [Mary's husband] got it a saterday night oh I believe I left my shawl at home my back shawl. I thought I had it in my carpet sack but when I got here it was not. i know i put it in. I opened the carpet sack to put my hym book in and maybe i laid it out and did not put it in again. I got a letter from Margaret M Claper saterday. I can write here with some comfort good Materials to write with. no children near I have a room to myself. old peter Magrue and polly lives with julie ann Kirk . . . Mrs. Dodd lives in the house at the taylor school house whare peter lived. well Almirea and Ann Barnet is just going in to town and I want to send this along so I must quit. tell Judith Ann to write soon give my love to the dear young folks at home tell Ruth [probably sister-in-law who lived near Mt. Vernon] I wish she was here

      your Mother Margaret Hardgrove

Wounded Arrive at Massillon Depot

In Tennessee, Henry's regiment experienced personal interaction with locals as they encountered plantation life. In vivid detail, he wrote to his brother William in Mt. Vernon about conversations which revealed different slants on slavery and "Secesh" issues. Meanwhile, families awaited money that should have arrived in Canton, but did not. Wounded soldiers returned to Massillon for treatment, and Margaret, herself, engaged in a talk with a soldier on the street in Massillon.

Union Station Tenn.
June 16 '62
Mr. William Hardgrove
Dear Brother

We have been traveling so much for the last two weeks that we could not write a letter or send them away if we had them written. We left Camp Shellwater near Corinth road the 2nd for Purdy.

We started bout three o'clock in the afternoon. Our Brigade was in the rear. I had command of the rear guard.

We had not gone far when it commenced raining as <u>usual</u>. *We seldom start on a march unless it rains; if it has not rained for two weeks before. The roads soon become so slippery that we had to encamp for the night. I put out my guard on picket. I run the picket line so as to take a log cabin into the line. After I got through placing my picket I went up to the log cabin knocked at the door. A soldier inside spoke up and said the house was full and they had all gone to bead. I tole them they were outside the picket line and I would arrest every one of them if they did not get up and let me in when they found out who I was they let me in. When I went in I found five or six boys out of our regiment drying their wet clothes around a big fire place and a Butternut [young Negro] getting supper for them.*

The boys invited me to take supper with them stay all night which I should have done without the invitation.

After supper I went to bead and slep soundly till morning. For the first time for six month I pulled off my clothes and went to bead citizen stile. I had a very good feather bead to sleep in.

I will give you a description of the Shantie. It was a log hut 10 by 12. A big awkward loom in the middle of the house which filled it most up. Two beads in one end, a place for an up stairs but none there except a few clapboards over the bead where I slept. It was a wet ugly night and the soft "platter of the soft rain over head" made me forget all the horrors of war and I was soon dreaming of "the girl I left behind me."

It was the house of a widow and when she saw our troops coming she got frightened and left for one of her neighbors houses. She sent the Butternut over to take care of the house and make all the money and [off?] the soldiers he could, which they are all eager to do. After he got things straitened up after supper he left with a promise to be back early in the morning to get breakfast for us. About daylight our friend Mr. Butternut made his appearance and informed us that breakfast was waiting for us at his house which was abut a quarter of a mile off after getting a

breakfast of warm coffee milk buisket and meat we paid
half a dollar a piece and left. We then began to travel
through a little better country than we had been used to
traveling through in this state.

After traveling ten miles we marched into the very
beautiful little village of Purdy which is the county seat of
McNary County and consists of about one thousand
inhabitants when it is prospering but there is not the half of
that many there now. After the band playing them several
national airs and letting the glorious old flag wave over
their county seat we marched out of town one mile and
camped for the night. I had got too good a taste of the
feather bead too sleep on the wet ground that night so an
other Lieut. and I broke for a house which we found not
over a mile from camp engaged our supper and lodging.
The man of the house had been in the Rebel Army most one
year and had got out on a sick furlow. I had a good bead to
sleep in and and a good breakfast in the morning.

The next day after a march of four miles we came to
the Mobile and Ohio railroad. There is a little place there
by the name of Bethel of ten or twelve buildings.

One regiment out of our Brigade remained there to
guard the place and repair the railroad. While our regiment
was resting there Sergeant Steffa and I went into the

country two or three miles came to a fine looking plantation went into the house and found a good union woman she got us a very good dinner. That day we got into the Pine Forest where I saw some of the largest pine trees I ever saw. The next day we traveled through very good country. The next day we began to get into Slavery proper.

The first plantation we came to was a very large one. They worked 140 slaves. It was a beautiful farm. The house was situated a heigh elevation. It was a large frame house well finished with a large yard in front and ful of shrubery.

One one end of the yard was the negro huts and the doors and windows blockaded with little urchins of all sizes.

The lady of the house made her appearance at a large window and her three fair haired daughter s at an other. The owner of the plantation came out to the road. He was Secesh to the hilt. We had taken his son prisoner the day before. He was a Lieut. in the Rebel Army.

Half a mile from the house we crossed the Memphis and Charleston railroad and the Hatchey river which is navigable for steam boats in time of heigh water.

One mile from the river we marched into one of the prittiest towns of its size that I have seen. Bolivar is the name it is the county seat. The buildings are very neat and some of the residences are very large.

The town is mostly inhabited by planters. The population is about one thousand.

While we were marching through the place but few of the natives made their appearance. Strong Secesh. We marched through the town and went into camp in a beautiful little clover field close to town. We got there Friday; sunday I went to church. *They treated me well gave me a good seat but the women turned up their noses at the Yankee Boys. Before we left we began to turn the opinion of the ladies with regard to the Yankees. They call us all Yankees down here. Since I was writing the above I had to quit and take command of a foraging party. I had four wagons and twenty men, we went out a little over a mile come to a secesh plantation. I filled the four wagons with corn and returned. The Old Boy took it very cool but was not willing to take the oath of alleigiance to receive his pay. To return on our march. We left Bolivar Tuesday morning and marched 7 miles through a very good country except water was scarce. At night we were very tired and encamped near a big spring which our men appreciated very much as they had hardly any all day and traveling through a cloud of dust and the sun hot enough to melt. The next morning we soon came to a little place by the name of Summerville the county seat of _____ and situated on the Mississippi Central railroad. It contains about seven or eight hundred inhabitants. The next day we drove into this place nine miles from Memphis. Union Station is the name of the place. It contains fifteen or twenty buildings and is on the Memphis and Louisville railroad. We expect to leave here soon for Memphis.*

Wheat harvest is about over. Aples are ripe and plenty of them. As I expect to go to Memphis early in the morning I will have to bring my poorly and huridly written letter to a close. Let me hear from you soon. I have not heard from home since the 1st of May [No signature]

Camp near MemphisTenn.

June 25, '62

Mr. Wm. Hardgrove

Dear Brother

I believe that I wrote to you a few days go while we were at Union Station.

We have been here most two weeks. We are encamped one mile and a half from the City in the Fair Ground. It is rather a poor place to camp. A poor shade and water scarce.

As we were about the first of the infantry troops here it is generaly believed we will stay here all summer and there is some talk of us going to Arkansas.

Memphis is a well built City some as fine buildings as I ever saw its population is about 30000.

The union feeling is becoming stronger evry day. Union flags are floating in evry direction over the City.

I just came in off of picket this morning. Our picket extended through a very thickly settled country outside of the corporation. There was some of the finest residences I have ever seen. They are mostly men that have retired from businesses. They are all strong Rebels. our outward post was in a splended yard full of beautiful shrubery of all kinds and beautiful shell and gravil walks. I went into the house it was furnished with the very best of everything. A negro brought me a glass of water on a very fine silver waiter. I had a long talk with the lady of the house. She was a strong Secesh but veery reasonable. I called at an other fine residence across the way from the last one. The lady of the house was a widow woman and a strong unreasonable Rebel.

We had some very lively talk on the important Subject. She claimed that the Rebel troops drove us into the river at Pittsburg landing; and that it was through Floyeds treachery that we took Fort Donelson. She said one of their Rebel generals had been in our camp the night befor the surender. I went back to see her again and from some cause she was wonderfully changed. Almost Union. I like to visit them in their splended mansions and taut them. I claim to be an abolitionist and tell them the slave is as good as they.

It is amusing to hear them tell how well they use their slaves and before we get done talking with them they will abuse them in some shape. We are right among them now, the regular old he kind [confusing wordage] and can talk to them about their institutions and they dare not resent it only in argument, and that we can beat them at. I am not very well today and make more mistakes than I get right. I have had a very bad cold for some time.

It is so warm here that when I am on duty I sweat till my clothes are all we then lay down with them on at night and catch cold. Our company is in good health now only one man sick.

We live well here now. All kind of vegitables are here in abundance. Green corn has ben coming into the camp for the last few days.

I rec'd a letter from mother today. She says Uncle John Jackson is dead.

Your Brother   Lieut. J. H. Hardgrove

N. B. Direct to Memphis Tenn.
I will send you ten cents of the Southern Shinplaster. It is
loosing its value evry day United State money goes as well
as gold here.

Massillon   June 22nd   62 Mr. Wm. Hardgrove
Dear son I will write a few lines this evening to let you
know the events of last week I believe that I have written to
you every week since I have been here george [Archer] got
a letter from Henry last fryday they ware at Dover tenn
[Tennessee] when he wrote but I understand they are at
Memphis now Henry sent george [Archer] a certificate to
get his mony he will get it at Canton, four hundred and fifty
dollars but the mony has not come yet. thare has been
several went to canton to get the money that there friends
sent the order for but could not get it when the mony comes
they will be notafied Henry wrote to george to send twenty
five dollars to Mt vernon to you by express george says it
will cost fifty cent to express it and he thinks he had beter
send it by letter. george [Archer] is going to let Doxey have
Henrys mony on interest till Henry wants it. Henry wrote to
Archer [still referring to Henry's brother-in-law] to let me
have 25 or 30 dollars or more if I wanted it I dont want so
much at one time but I can get what I do need at any time I

have only had one letter from Henry since I have ben here I mail a letter to him yesterday and sent him twenty five cents worth of postage stamps he wants george to send him a dollars worth of stamps they cant get thare as cheap as they can here. I stayed at Archers all last week went down to town [Massillon] yesterday evening last night Hariet and Minerva both slipt off while I was in the kitchen washing the super dishes and did not come back till nine oclock orrick come and him and me talked a while and Hariet come home she had been over to Mungs [possibly Mong's, a Massillon business]. Minerva was over at [Sharlot] stellings this morning orrick was thare early. he was going to orville [Orrville, Ohio] he askd Hariet if she would go with him to orrvill he got a splendid buggy and team so he got sharlot steling Hiram and Hariet a bran new two seated buggy they started quite early. I went to church Minerva come up to Marys and benets [Hardgrove cousin] wife come with her after church I come up and after super george, Mary and the children went to take a buggy ride sally [possibly Clapper family neighbor] and Minerva went home. Almirea [Mary Archer's step-daughter] went to take a horse back ride and here I am writing. nobody but my self. I just now went out and got some plantain leaves for the rabits they like that better than any else I believe the poor things half starves when I ant here I feed them three or four times a day Hariet has moved some of her things they will get them all moved this week I must go back thare tonight and it is geting late now sundown and I will have to quit writing you can get this a wednesday and write by the next mail or If you could sent it to Mt. vernon I could get it by saterday. I have an opertunity to hear from Henry often. so many coming home sick or wounded. Dr. Hurxstall has come home and brot two poor wounded boys with him from corinth one has his arm shot of and the other his leg yes thare is three of them . . . his [3rd soldier] shot through the hip they are at the American house [hotel in downtown Massillon]. yesterday as I went down to town I met a returned soldier and had a talk with him he was a regular Just from corinth the town is full of soldiers thare was one at our church today he come from western virginia a Nephew of Daniel perkeys his mother is a widow.

    give my respects to Mrs. Mast, frank and ann and my love to Ruth and all the dear young folks at home.

    good night and god bless and protect you

       your Mother
       M Hardgrove

4th of July

A Fourth of July glimpse by Margaret highlights traveling by canal boat as celebrations were kicked off in Navarre and Massillon. Lots of other exciting things happening as July unfolds: George Archer got an offer for his iron hownds from local businessman/inventor Joseph Davenport. Margaret offered advice ranging from what George should do with patent dollars to what should be done with Gen. McClellen! At the same time, Henry's Fourth was remembered mainly by just remembering. Later, he entered into one of the finest areas in Memphis and wished his mother could come and visit. Even while she considered such a fantastic adventure, a very special tin box found its way home.

Massillon   July 6th 62   Mr. William Hardgrove
Dear Son I am here at Marys this morning the sun is so hot
I could not go to church the last three days have been
extremely warm the odd fellows had a prosession in Nevar
[Navarre, Ohio] the fourth. thare was a great many from
town went I had thought of going but concluded it would be
too hot to go on a crowded canal boat the sun would be too
hot to stay on Deck and to stay down in the cabin with such
a crowd would be worse so I staid at home with Hariet we
had a good super had some company for super we had
some fine large cucumbers brot from pittsburg and at night
we enjoyd the amusements that was going on the fire works
from one end of the town [Massillon] to the other the sky
Rockets were whising up sky high george got your letter
last week but he has not got the mony yet thare is a great
many that has orders to receive mony at canton but they
could not pay the order til they got the list of names from
the war department or some other place george says it can
be got in a few days last monday evening I saw Gilberthorp
Erel [Earl] in town he had just come from canton he had an
order for eighty dollars from george [his soldier son
George Earl] but he could not tell when he could get the
mony. Archer has made a good thing by his iron howns he
has been offerd ten thousand dolars for his right last week

with good security but some of his advisors tells him to

hold on by seling county rights he can make more than

fifteen thousand he asked me last night what I would advise

him to doo I told him to take the ten thousand he might find

some trouble in colecting if he sold county rights.

I got a letter from Henry last week he was very unwell he

had been suffering from the effects of a cold for more than

two weeks he was not able for Duty when he wrote he was

Doctoring himself I am afraid he will have got to Richmond

yet or maybe they have gone as gen McClellen has got his

big army all killd off what was not killd or taken prisnors

have backd out and now they will call the western troops

thare to take Richmnd or get killd. gen McClellen is either

a coward or a traitor he has cost our government more

than ninty thousand such men as him are worth I wish the

rebels would take him prisenor and hung him the news

come here last night that McClellens army had been

surounded and taken prisnors forty thousand all thare

cannon and everything.

Thare is no news aloud to come in the papers from the

army Harriet has got in her new house it is much

pleasanter than it was down in the old brick [house].

george he says Davenport offers him ten thousan dollars

pay part in hand and the balance in one year for his pattent with good security. now I am anxious to hear from home. I have got a new shawl very fine black moreno seven dollars as well a new gingham dress a pair of black prunel gaiters. I would like to know how sister susans health is and I am glad to hear that your health has been so good. Minerva was out at Deans last week they live about a mile from here I dont know if she will stay another week or not yesterday morning Hariet and me come up here and after diner Rebecka and Mrs. Hoover [neighbors] came in. the strawberrys are nearly gone but thare is plenty of cherrys both sweet and sour and thare will be lots of pears let me hear from you some

your Mother   M Hardgrove

Camp near Memphis Tenn.
July 5 '62
Mr. William Hardgrove
Dear brother:

Being at leasure today I thought I would write you a few lines to let you know how we spent the Fourth in "Dixie" In the morning a few rounds were fired by the field pieces and one or two regiments of infantry fired a round of blank cartridges.

All was quiet then til noon in camp except now and then a fancy load of women of the City would drive through the camp with flying colors.

At noon the batteries which are five or six in number and six in each battery opened out. Each battery fired 34 rounds. At night the battteries opened out again. The infantry pitched in furiously and to close up the Fourth we had a good deal of martial noise, which brought to rememberance scenes of bygone days on the plains of Shiloh and Fort Donelson. There was much wanting to represent the reality. The clear ring which the iron ball gives to the report was wanting. And the hideous noise which the long shot and shell made in their passage through the air.

After the fireing was over Lieut. Col. Woods made a short speech to our regiment. It was short and spicy.

After that was over I went up to the City and an old Rebel drank a toast to the old Rebel Jef Davis the consequence was he was put in the lockup and his house burnt to ashes. A mob was feared and our regiment slept on their arms all night to be ready to put it down.

All is quiet today and very warm. There is a general Courts-marshal at head quarters. One 1st Lieut. of Co. B our regiment is having his trial. they have several charges against him the first charge against him for which he was put under arrest was refusing to take his company out in drill one afternoon. He and his company had just come in off the picket, it had been customary after a company coming in off of picket duty to have the rest of the day to themselves. The Col ordered him out. He refused to go. The Col. ordered him under arrest and his confinement was limited to his company quarters. He broke over the lines for which an other charge was prefered against him. It is believed he will cashered.

Lieut. Blackburn made a narrow escape. He was relieved from arrest yesterday morning He has been under arrest for four or five weeks. While we were at Bolivar he was Officer of the camp guard He got a little too much intoxicated to navigate properly for which he was put under arrest.

If the charges had not been withdrawen he would have been casheered. The Col. is afraid of our company or I think he would have stuck Marsh. Our boys are in good health with one exception. One of our men is in the hospital but is getting better.

Our camp is about a quarter of a mile from the river.

Oposite our camp and one mile below the City the river makes a short bend. In the bend of the river is a large island 7 or 8 miles long and from a half to two miles wide. Close to the island lies the reck of the Rebel ram Beauregard. Above the City lies an other. Union sentiment is gaining ground very fast.

I wrote you a letter while were at Bolivar shortly after we were paid off that I think you have not got. I have now written you four or five letters and only rec'd one dated June 23rd.

I sent my money to Archer by sutter who went home I tole Archer to send you twenty give dollars

Your brother
Lieut. J. H. Hardgrove

Fort Pickering Memphis Tenn.
July 19 '62
76 reg. O.U. st
Mr. William Hardgrove

Dear brother: it has not been more than a week since I wrote the last letter to you, since I have not rec'd a letter from any one at home

Being at leasure this morning I thought I would write you a few lines to keep you posted of our whereabouts.

We are still in the old Fort with a prospect of remaining for some time, if I may judge from appearances.

We have about one thousand negroes working on the entrenchments and cutting down tress. Since war has spread its wide desolation over Memphis it hardly looks like the same place it did when we first came.

We are encamped in a beautiful grove in what might be called the suberbs of the City although we are outside of the Corporation. For miles out in the country it is so thickly settled as a country village. The Contrabands are cutting the trees down in evry direction and falling them so as to make it impassable and impossible for an army to surprise us. or whip us without a vast superior force.

We are makeing the heaviest ind of entrenchments, amounting almost to fortifications. The ditch is fifteen feet wide and eight feet deep. We take advantage of the ground regardless of residences buildings or anything else.The entrenchments pass through some splendid yards. It makes the old Rebels look with vengence.

Where our regiment stands picket is right through where the wealthiest part of the citizens of the City live.

There are some or many of the finest dwellings I ever saw. It is a beautiful place.

They live in grand stile. While I am on picket i have lots of fun with them, some of them being desireous of knowing what a Yankee is will invite me into their house to find out wheather we really are "Human beings." I was on picket the other day; A young lawyer that lives wit his sister a young widow in a splended residence invited me in to have a talk. They treated me with all the respect they could. They were all fond of talking and particularly to a live Yankee.

The trouble was they all wanted to talk at once. They were mighty strong Secesh but I held them level, while I was with them and when I left I had to promise to come back and see them. Which I will certainly do the first time I am on picket.

The young widow is a beautiful lady. They have some mighty good looking women here but they have nothing else to do but cultivate that part. She was telling me how kind she used one of our wounded captains that was taken prisoner at Shiloh. They use our officers well that they take prisoners but the privates have a hard time among them.

We are closing in on them here by degrees. I will send you a Memphis paper with the general orders in. read them and you will see what kind of chance we give them. property is being confiscated every day more or less and rebel families leaving the City.

We are making good use of the negroes. Wallace is doing what Jim Lane was going to do with his men give each one a servant. We drill one hour in the evening and ay in the shade the rest of the day while the negroes are doing the work. Our company have one to cook for them. We still have the one we brought from Massillon Jo Clemons.

For some time we have had such a small force here that we have been expecting an attack evry day. Yesterday Sherman's Divisions came in which will make us strong enough to give them a big fight should they feel disposed to give us a call some of these fine cool days. Our boys are all "spilin" for a fight and would rather fight than eat but would like to eat a little first particularly if it was eating time. We have lively times now. Campbell's Renowned Minstrels have been here for some time. But we have all the negro performance we want with the Contrabands. At night they have big times, dances, singing prayer meeting and all kind of amusement. They all think they will be free which I think so too if they go ahead with the negro question at Washington.

Wallace is in favor of giving them arms which you will see if you read his speech at Washington.

We have plenty of newspapers we get the Cincinnati Daily Commercial and many other northern papers in two days from the time of publication

Your brother
Lieut. J. H. Hardgrove

Massillon   July 19th 62   Mr. Wm Hardgrove
Dear son I intended to write home yesterday but I had to finish a letter I had commenced to John Richard [O.J.'s young son] to California [probably the small town of California 3 miles north of Brownsville, Pennsylvania] and write to Henry and while I was writing to Henry Minerva came and brot me a letter from him he wants me to come to memphis to see him. he is well he has had a bad cold but has recovered his health he says he thinks I would injoy the trip very much if I would come I should get a hundred dollars of his mony get on the cars and go to cincinati thare was a boat left cincinati every morning he says the scenery down the Ohio and Missippi is grand and beautiful and

why may I not take some pleasure in my old age while the lamp still burns. well thare is several reasons why I could not go conveniently at this time the first is george has not got Henrys mony yet and the second reason is I would be afraid the Rebels might fire in to the boat a ball from one of them big guns pasing through the boat might alarm me a litle bit but if I had company from home with me either male or female I would go he says I can stay at one of the best houses in Memphis and have darkeys to wait on me and he will send a contraband home with me either male or femal he says they have everything they want to eat green corn cucumbers beets radishes cabage/squashes.

I have written so many letters that i have run out of paper orrick was going down to town a saterday evening was to get some paper but he met with an acident and he did not go after he eat his super he went out and comencd a romp with almira [Mary Archer's 16-year-old step-daughter daughter]. he held her with one hand and went to pump water with the other and the pump handle flew up wth such force it smashd his nose his eyes are very black and sweld so he did not go to town and I only had three sheets of paper a sunday. one sheet and half of this I sent to Henry one orrick wrote to Henry and I will have to wait til tomorrow to get more paper. george has cut part of his wheat it is very heavey but injured some with the rust they are going to cut the rest of it this afternoon his wheat is not injured with rust he says now. they have a great many cherrys and the largest I ever saw we have ben very busey taking the seeds out and caning Mary has put up six gallon in glass jars and stone jars I have been seeding cherrys this two days Hariet went down to the farm last fryday and made her curnt jelly an cand up carnation cherrys. Andrew Bahney came home from California a saterday he has been gone eight or ten years—crack I wont have to complain for want of paper orrick has just brot me a quarter ream or one hundred sheets. now my friends if I have any can hear from me. I doo not know yet when that mony of Henrys can be had or what is the reason it is not paid I will inquire of some one that can give me some information for george either does not know or does not care. Mary and me was going up to Earls [Ruth and Gilbert Earl] today and I would ask him as he has an order for george earls mony but they broke the buggy last night coming home from the shop they will mend it today it raind hard this morning

thare is great many women that are expecting mony at canton [Canton, Ohio] george says they go to canton every few days but are disappointed I think it is a great imposition or swindle on the people. Henry said thare

64

regiment sent home elevn thousand dollars and I believe
some boddy is puting the interest of that mony in thare
pocket. Archer has a plan to get Henry home a while he
thinks Henry could get leave of absence to come home to
raise a company but I doo not believe he can at this time
when thare is so much need of all the men they have in the
service the Rebels have had such a good success latey that
they are more bold than ever. I am anxious to hear how
susan is her health was so bad when yo wrote last I left my
thimble in the pocket of my dress if you found it take care of
it I cant say yet when I will be at home rite soon. they talk
of drafting Militia. If they doo I hope some of these sesech
sympathizers will have to go for they are so provokingly
imprudent Mary has three young pee fowls your Mother

M Hardgrove

[Added to her letter, written by candle light same evening]
I have to add another line to say that george told me this
eveing he believed the soldiers mony had come to canton
andI supose he will send you yours as soon as he gets it he
has gone down to town [Massillon] tonight and orrick and
Almira [Mary and George Archer's 16-year-old daughter]
has gone to Barnets to a party Mary got a letter from
Henry this evening he sent his epaulets home.he sent them
to New Arck [probably Newark, Ohio] by a sutler and he

expressd them home to Massillon to george [Archer] they have been here two or three weeks and none of us had wrote to Henry that they had come and he wanted to know whether they had come or not they were sent in a tin box lind [lined] with canton flanel and lapt [probably wrapped] in coten wading they are beautiful articals they came safe. I am writing by candle and it is after ten oclock I had come in to go to bed and thought I would write a line and here come Mary. Almeda [Almira Archer?] had ben in bed and got sick and vomited all over cordelia and Mary come in to get dry cloths for them. george and phil [possibly Archer farm hand] has come back and now I believe they are all in bed. Charly [posssibly farm hand] got hurt badly the day before yesterday he was in the wood house on top of the wood which was piled up very hight he was puling at a stick to get it out and fell backward to the ground it knocked the breath out of him and for a while we thought it was all over with Charly he is very sore in his back and breast since but will soon be all right well I must quit and go to bed. this is the gleaning of the paper next time I will have a hole sheet I have wrote in such a hurry I dont know if you can read it good night

Margaret Hardgrove

Camp Helena, Arkansas

It was a hot August of the regiment's discontent at their camp near Helena, Arkansas. In letters to his brother William and sister-in-law Julie Ann, Henry wrote of illnesses, increased cases of desertions and a nasty colonel. Some of their regimental units had headed to Vicksburg with a large gun boat, while some remained at camp constantly digging trenches. Henry was all for "less digging and more fighting," so they could help end the war and go home.

Camp near Helena Arkansas
August 6, '62
Mr. William Hardgrove

Dear brother:

I received your letter of yesterday it found me convalescent. I have not been well since we have been here. I had a chance at the ague for four or five days.

I have missed it for two days and I think if I take good care of myself I will not have it any more. Blackburn and I both had the ague.

The Captain is at home on furlow. The sickly season has commenced. Our regiment has good health so far.

There are about twenty in the hospital from our regiment but none from our company. Although there are several that are not well.

There is a good deal of disatisfaction among the soldiers about the negroes.

(Henry's letter comes to a halt here.)

August 8
Since I wrote the above I have had two more turns of the feaver. Night before last I had a very high feavor; last night I had a slight feaver enough to keep me awake till after midnight. It is an intermittant feavor it commences in the evening about sundown and lasts till after midnight. I

am taking Homeapathey medicine. Through the day time I feel very well and sometimes I can eat a very hearty meal.

Now about the "Scout" W. S. Lathan. From what I can find out he is an imposter and should be arrested himself. He came to our regiment when we were close to Corinth. He had some traps to sell which was generaly believed he had stolen. That was the last we saw of him. I read what you wrote to me about him to Adjutant Miller and he is of the same opinion of him that I am. He thinks he is a deserter from some regiment. I would not have much to do with him he may be right but I have my doubt about him being genuine. We were paid off the other day. we receive two months. I am going to send home one hundred dolars the first chance I get. I wont send any more home by the State Agent. The last letter I got from Massillon they had not drawn it. I will send it by express as soon as I can get to town if they have an express office there. There is a good deal of desertion going on in the regiment. Four men from our company have deserted.

Nothing more but

remain Your brother

Lieut. J. H. Hardgrove

Camp near Helena Arkansas

August 11 '62

Mr. William Hardgrove

Dear Brother: I will write you a few lines this morning to let you know that I expressed one hundred dollars to you. I sent it to Mt. Vernon.

Take what I owe you out of it and use the rest for anything you want.

I told George Archer to send you what I owed you but I expect he has not drawn it. The last account I had of it they had not drawn it.

I still have the intermittant feaver. Last night it was very light. If I could get a transfer to the 104th regiment i would take it if for nothing else but to get home for a while. This is a regular feaver and ague country. There is a good deal of dissatisfaction among the soldiers of our regiment About 50 have deserted. Five have desert from our Company. While we were in Tenessee several deserted. They were arrested and had their trial in columbus and were cleared. It has had a good effect to start others to desert. together with the meanness of the Coll. he uses his men so mean I would not blame them if they would all desert. Other regiments here have no camp guard. Our old drunken Col. made over one hundred of his men stand guarding in the hot sun all day around the camp. He does it because he is mad at the men and wants to punish them. It only makes the men hate him and soldiering the more and they will desert and pass through his strong camp guard in spite of him.

I have not heard from home since I have been in this camp which is two weeks. Let me hear from you as soon as you get this.

Your Brother

Lieut. J. H. Hardgrove

Camp near Helena Arkansas

Sunday morning August 24 '62

Mrs. J. A. [Judith Ann] Hardgrove [Henry's sister-in-law]

Dear sister: I received your letter and Williams of the 18th day before yesterday and was very glad to hear form you as I had not heard from any of you for some time. I am glad to hear of you haveing such good crops but you have had a very poor time of getting them in. soldiering must go ahead if the plough stands.

I think we have been wonderfully favored with a good harvest this year when it is most needed. I still have the ague I have got it into a shape now that I something about it. It comes evry three days int he evening. I am takeing nothing but quinene bark in whiskey once a day.

This evening will be my time for it again. It has brought me down to 138 lbs. less than I have weighed for 10 years.

If I can get a leave of absence I go home this fall. I am hardly sick enough to get one now. The old Quack in our regiment wont sign a certificate unless he thinks they will die before they get home.

The regiment has been gone eight days. We have not heard from it sin they left. Two days more and their rations will be out as they only started with ten days. They may be down about Vicksburg as a large gun boat fleat went along with them. I think we will soon be doing something here as the hot weather will soon be over. It is geting more pleasant than it was a few weeks ago. We are very eager for the war to close and are waiting patiently for the new volenteers to get into the field than if the rebellion is not put down imeadiately I shal get discouraged. Our army has not been too timerous and scarey.

We have been building too many breastworks. Our Army can be tracked through the south by the breastworks they have been building.

At Shiloh after we whiped them and was afterward reinforced to double our number we commenced building breastworks like a lot of cowards.

We had the largest army that has been together at one time during the war an army big enough to have marched strait through to the gulf and whiped the whole Southern Confederacy, yet we moved forward at a snails gallop building one line of breastworks after an other till we got into Corinth.

We had an army of nearly two hundred thousand men and afraid to march on to fifteen thousand Rebels without building breastworks. I go in for less diging and more fighting. what if we do loose more men by rushing the war. we will eventually loose the men by sickness if it is prolonged and make the men dig dichs instead of fighting.

Diging so many ditches only makes coward out of the men. Enough of that. If the regiment does not return soon I will try to get hoe. The Captain has not come back. He has been gone one month. He got a leave of absence of twenty days and got it extended twenty days more.

I wrote William a letter after sending him the hundred dollars by express. He did not say anything about getting it. I suppose it had not come.

I cannot write as much as intended to. I had the ague hard last night. I am going up to see the surgeon this morning to see if he will sign a certificate for a leave of absence.

Yours truly

Lieut. J. H. Hardgrove

Not a Chicken Safe in Massillon

Tension reigned over the Village of Massillon and surrounding countryside. Margaret and folks back home were dealing with 109th and 115th regiments building barracks and camping there. Word was that not a solitary chicken was safe any more! In Arkansas, Henry reported things were looking "gloomy and mysterious." General Steel had just taken command.

Massillon   Aug 22   '62   Mr. Wm. Hardgrove

Dear son I received your letter and if I go after sally
[perhaps a relative of William's wife who has been visiting
the area] I would like to go in two weeks for I want to come
home two or three weeks oh I have made a mistake I mean
in a few weeks. John Beamer was here at the camp he staid
all night in camp and come up to Archers in the morning he
only staid an hour or two. I did not see him he came to see
some of thomas hawkins [family with close Hardgrove
associations going back to Pennsylvania] boys that are in
camp. the 109 reg leaves a sunday the 115 will stay ere a
while it is not safe of a man to talk sausy now. sighsi
[unclear spelling] young got beaten badly and had to give
his note for one hundred dollars and he sent it down and
five dollars more to treat the soldiers or they would have
distroyd his house he has built a new barn one hundred and
thirty feet long. I have just now heard that a letter from
Michel Hardgrove says the 76 reg has left Helena and
Henry is left thare sick. we have had two letters from him
since he was at Helena in which he said he was sick. he
wanted me to send him a feather pillow which we did we
put one in the box and I think capt briggs got to Helena
yesterday or the day before. his wife [Captain Brigg's wife]
got a letter from him at cincinati he would leave thare on

fryday at noon and by wedensday he would arrive at Helena I see in the dayly com the 76 reg had left on a chase after a party of Rebels which they met and captured so me and the rest ran away and they had returned before capt Briggs would get here. Capt B sayd he would get Henry a bed in cincinati they are made with sacking with the head raisd *like a lounge and can be folded up they have light frames he sayd he would get one for himself and one for Henry he has chill feaver. the governer is to be here at camp tomorrow (saterday) and a sunday the 109 leavs and the 115 stays I understood they ware going to organise thare reg here if so when this reg leaves thare will another come. they have built baracks and are still puting up more every day the people here may be glad when they are gone. thare will not be a chicken goose or turkey left in the Neiborhood. they stole 18 of Marys [Mary Archer lived on Pigeon Run Road]³¹ chickens in one night she had her young chickens and a few of the old ones and the white gobler shut up in the wood house and they are all she has left. Mrs Delia Hay is at Hiram Bahneys she came thare a tuesday. I come up here yesterday morning. Mary was in town and I come up with her in the waggon. Delia sayd she came from virginia. I dd not ask her any questions yet but I will. she will be here tomorrow. we will all be down at*

77

camp tomorrow as governor tod [Gov. David Tod of Ohio] is to be thare. Brother Martin [possibly church friend] was at Hariets last fryday Hariet and Mrs. Caly came up to Marys. I had come up a Tuesday and I went to town with them I had two letters to Mail one to J A [William's wife Julie Ann] and one to Henry. I stopt at Benets and at the p o [post office] and Hariet went on home and when I went home here I found Billey Martin. He staid all night and the next day he went up to camp came back in the evening staid till after night said he was going to Doxeys bid good night and in five minits he returnd and staid all night. a sunday Minerva and I went to hear him preach. Hariet and Hiram went out in the country to Folts,s. finaly Martin staid till tuesday I think he is as lazy as ever. he wants to be a chaplain in the 115 reg he lives in a little town five miles from Aliance. I forget the name. if you send mony to me to fech sally I think I will go toward the the last of the week after next and then I will go home. Minerva wants to go home with me. I dont expect you will get this till wednesday your Mother M Hardgrove

Camp near Helena Arkansas

Sept. 9 '62

Mr. Wm. Hardgrove

Dear Brother I received a letter form you a few days ago which I will answer. My health is improving very fast. I have got the Ague broke up and a good appetite in its place. The Capt. [Briggs] came back one week ago last Sunday. He brought me two boxes of things mostly caned fruit and dried fruit came in vey good time just as I was getting over the Ague.

I never heard of the death of Capt. Edgar before you wrote to me. I have not heard of an officer's death since war began that I regret as much. I believe all Jo wanted was the practice and he would be qualified for one of the heighest offices in the Army. I cant help but think he was a good officer and well liked by his men. I saw an account of the fight but no names of the killed. They must have had a hard fight.

Well our side of the questions at present looks very gloomy mysterious and almost discouraging. Whiped at evry point very bad indeed. but we have a little army down here of about 25000 men that will hardly turn their back on less than five times their number. all the men here are old soldiers and have all been in hard engagements and have prooved themselves pluck to the back bone.

We are not just 'zactly spilin' for a fight but we *would just as leave give them turn as not. When they give us a call they will find some mighty puff "chaps" to handle. A good portion of our army are germins. Segats old army are all here. There is no sign of a movement here yet. Gen. Steel is command here now. Curtis has been ordered to report at Washington. We are well supplied with artilery and cavelry of the best kind. I received a letter from mother this morning of the 3rd. George Earl has been sick with a feaver and a bad cough. He is better. He had a fight with one of the men and got whiped which I think caused his sickness.*

We are begining to live very well again. Vegitables are coming to camp. we can get fresh bread in town potatoes, cabbage tomatoes, and chickens are worth 37 1/2 cts. per head. potatoes three dollars pr. barrel.

The health of the Army is generly good.

My note for $25 was in your last letter.

I tried to get a furlow but could not. So I come to conclusion I had better get well. I put quinine double doses.

Your brother

Lieut. J. H. Hardgrove Co. II 76 reg. O.V. II

Camp near Helena Arkansas

Sept. 18 '62

Mr. William Hardgrove

Dear Brother I received your letter of the 3rd yesterday
which I will try and answer this morning.

      There has been nothing new occured in camp since
I last wrote to you with the exception of one brigade that
has gone to the assistance of Cincinnati, and this morning
two regiments of infantry and a bettery of artilery and a
battallion of cavelry that went down the river where they
are destined for I am unable to say.

      The report is here that the lower fleet is bombarding
Vicksburg. Since I wrote the above I was called in to go to
Helena with the Provost Guard. It was at Gen. Osterhouses
headquarters. I had 43 prisoners to guard. boys that were
picked up in town for getting drunk and other offences. A
little wild Irishman was brought in yesterday he was
covered with blood. three guards brought him in he came in
backward cursing and swearing. The guard had to knock
him down with the butt of their guns evry few minits to keep
him quiet. At night we had a big time the Provost Martial
was promoted from captain to major he opened two boxes
of wine and the dutch had a lively time drinking and

smoking and singing. a splended string band was on hand to surendade the Major.

This Army is nearly all dutch, but very few American regiments are here. Ours and a few others. I will send you a C.S.A. gun receipt which one of our boys got when they routed the 31st Lua. reg. at Milikins Bend. The Rebels dont leave a gun behind them of any description they take them and give the owners a receipt for them. Geo. Earl is still in the Hospital but is most well. My health is good and a spended appetite. I am glad I did not go down river with the expedition it cost the officers 40 or 50 dollars a piece. It was a regular drunken spree for the officers. the last night they were on the boat they got so drunk and made so much noise the privates had to quiet them down. At the same time their was a sick soldier died, on board the boat.

I received a letter from mother today. They getting very tired of the soldiers there. They have been steeling evrything they can get their hands on. That shows a want of deciplin in the Col. The fleet that went down with Rebel prisoners to exchange brought back one of our boys that was taken prisoner. He is very sick.

Your Brother

Lieut. H J. H. Hardgrove

Shoot the Captain!

As Autumn officially arrived in Massillon in 1862, Margaret found herself with a rare free day and, of course, took pen in hand. This time she wrote to her daughter-in-law, Judith Ann "Ann," who lived on a farm north of Mt. Vernon, Ohio. With end of summer visits, the Archers were figuring out how to help accommodate rides for departing visitors in their waggon with that of transporting hoggs! In Arkansas, Henry and his men also anxiously prepared to move. At last, relief from their everlasting camp experience where disease and emotional fatigue had taken its toll on the men. Sentences were being handed down for deserters.

Massillon   Sept 21st '62   Mrs. J A Hardgrove

Dear Ann [Judith Ann] not having anything to do to day
but to read and write I will trouble you with a few lines.
Ann [different Ann, possibly Margaret's daughter who lived
near Wiliam] left here last monday for Reamers and I have
just wrote a few lines to her she said she would probably
stay two weeks thare and orrick and george Archer was to
go in to Reamers after some hoggs that John Reamer has
bought for george. and orrick told Ann that she should stay
till they come and her and sally could come back with them
in the little waggon but george says he dont know when he
will get the time to go and he will put only one seat in the
waggon and a goods box in the hind part to put his two
hoggs in. so I wrote to Ann to come on the carrs when she
got her visit out. we got a letter yesterday from Henry but it
had been written the 8 of this month before they left
Helena. I see by the last monday paper they had left
Helena. he sayd he had got the ague broke he had not had
it for five or six days. he sent a sesesh letter home that the
boys had got while down the river on that expidition it had
been writen at the time of the batle on the chickhominy. I
think Ann will be back out here next week or the last of this
week and I cant set the day to come home till I see her and
I am geting home sick. I want to see the dear young folks at

84

home as soon as I can. I will let you know when we will be thare I would like to go next week but cant go till Ann comes back. Mary Reamer was here to see us her cousin Mary Ann smith was with her (formerly Hawkins). John Reamer had been here the week before. Henry says they got the things we sent them and every thing was good and I was glad they got them. we are going to brookfield [small community west of Massillon] this afternoon or I would write more [No signature this time]

Sept 27 '62   Mr. William Hardgrove
Dear son I write today to let you know that we expect to be home next saterday. this is saterday. Ann has not come back yet but I look for her today this pen is so bad I cant write I got a letter from Henry yesteray he was well. you must excuse me for not writeing more it is too bad to write with and I have not time to go down to get one til I take this down I think a saterday will be the third of october or the fourth [No signature this time]

Camp near Helena Arkansas
Sept 28 '62
Mr. William Hardgrove

Dear Bother as we are expecting orders to leave here evry day I thought I would write you a few lines before we left. Our army has been preparing for the last week or ten days. We are now ready to leave and have orders to march at the shortest notice. Where we are bound for I can not tell but judging from the moves made yesterday we will leave in the direction of Little Rock we will have two streams to cross, the white and another river. It is hard to tell where we will go. One thing we are well prepared with cartridges. We have eight thousand rounds of cartridges which will weigh over eight hundred pounds.

We are all ready to start and prefere marching to lying in camp. It is harder work to march but the men have better health. We have ben having a long rest here, over two months. Our Army here is in a good condition to do good service.

Although we have defeated the main body of the Rebels at Washington we have nothing to brag of. They balanced accounts with us at Harpers Ferry. The curses of the Ohio troops about old Tom Ford are not few. From the commercial of the 25 which we received today it is all quiet on the Potomac again. Our army is entirely to inactive.

More die of sickness from inaction than are killed inaction We have been here over two months and not less than three hundred have been burried here during that time and discharged. But once we get started we will not have any more complaint to make about an inactive life.

George Earl had got his discharge he has been sick for some time. It is more playing off than sickness.

One private has been discharged. They will start home in a few days.

This morning two men were drumed out of camp and two others sentenced to hard work in the Alton Penitentiary. One that was drummed out of camp threatened to shoot his captain. He had his head shaved drummed out of camp and dishonarably discharged from the U. S. Service.

The other one that was drummed out deserted got as far as Cairo and was arrested and sent back to his regiment.

He was sentenced to serve out the remainder of his time at hard labor in the Alton Penitentiar. The other two that were not drummed out sentenced to six months hard labor and forfeit 10 dollars a month of their pay. The charges against them were absent from their regiment without leave. Five men have deserted our Company. If we get them they will either be shot or drummed out of camp. I was taking a walk through Helena today. I visited the nunery and saw the black and white veiled sisters. There are seventeen sisters in the institution. It is a very nice place and from the size of the trees in the yard, which is full, it is an old place.

I did not go inside but if we stay here a week longer I will visit it again. It is along side of Gen. Hindman's residence consists of a new brick building well finished on the outside. There is a large front full of weeds. There is a large ridge running through the suburbs of the town on top of which our men have built a strong front and mounted several large size guns on it. I suppose mother is at your house by this time. I got letter from Mary Archer yesterday and she said mother was going to start the next week.

Your Brother
Lieut. J. H. Hardgrove

[Letter probably to William, likely written October, 1862]
I will go home this fall if I can get a furlow. The captain has a furlow written and will hand it in today.

It is a hard job to get one. Our Col. is to mean to start it right. It has to be signed by the Col. of our regiment by Gen. Grant and the Secretary of War.

I have found out who the Miller is you spoke of being in our regiment. He is acting Adjutant of the regiment, he was orderly or 1st sergeant in a company from Newark. He will receive the appointment soon. Charlie is a fine little fellow and makes a very good adjutant. There is strong talk of us going to Va. to help Mc. into Richmond. It is just the place we want to go. We have got our hand in a little and would sooner assist them than play it alone here. As soon as the hot weather is over we will have our hands full down here. In Arkansas they impressing every man that can shoulder a musket. This war is going to last longer than I thought it would. The fight at Richmond makes things look a little gloomy but not discouraging. We will whip them eventually but our defeat at Richmond, for I dont know what else to call it will encourage the Rebels. McClellan has got a better position but the trouble is he was forced to take it.

Gurrilla parties are scattered all thorough the country they come up to the picket but do it very sly and keep out of range of our French rifles which carry an ounce ball a thousand yards. I have a navy revolver (six shooter) that I got at Fort Donelson which will carry level half a mile. I can shot across the Mississipp river with it which is three quarters of a mile wide.

As sherman's Division is coming in it is likely I will get a chance to see him. I suppose you are having a big harvest. It has been very dry here. The corn does not look very well.

It grows about twice as tall here as it does north we have had rosten ears here for over a month. Peaches are here in abundance Watermellons are coming into market. If you remember of seeing it in the papers. The Rebels advised th farmers to plant lots of watermellons.

We expect to be paid off soon.

Let me hear form you soon.

Your brother
Lieut. J. H. Hardgrove

Horse Races, Hush-Hush

Margaret's letter to her son in Mt. Vernon, Ohio, bubbled with excitement about Massillon, Canton and Wooster fairs. Her favorite, the horse races, was something to keep hush-hush, however. There had been a long spell with no word from home to Henry that October and November. For several weeks, there had been 1 or 2 funerals every day in Massillon, keeping Jo Bahney's hearses on the go. In a rare sign of Margaret's anxiety, she dreamed of receiving letters from her son William. Alas, she awoke before contents were revealed! As Henry penciled another note from aboard the "Campion," he told of passing the wreck of his old transport "The Universe" and looking forward to returning home for good.

Massillon   October 11th '62   William Hardgrove

Dear son I promist to write last week but owning to
surrounding circumstances I could not almira [Mary and
George Archer's 16-year-old daughter] is geting better. the
other children are well Minerva has been with Hariet til
tuesday evening lizzy Heldenbran come for her. Hariet and
me was out to old Mr. Bahneys a sunday. a tuesday I went
to Mr Doxeys he was not at home but he come up to
Hirams [son-in-law] and we talkd the subject over and I
found the whole trouble was that sam Bowman had kept the
25 cents that I had paid him for Mr. Doxey. The election is
over and the unterified democracy has one up salt crick.
the republican Majority in Massillon was over a hundred
and 70. they had the best fair here they ever had and thare
was a right smart chance of horse racing I looked on and
injoyd the sport admirally [admirably]but don't tell aunt
susy though. I neither tore my dress nor bett my mony.. O J
and J H [posssibly cousin John M. Hardgrove of
Butterbridge family] went to wooster to the fair and
Minerva went to canton to the fair. Mary wants to go home
with me or I would go home next week and I doubt if she
goes if I doo wait for her. she says the week after next we
can go and I will whether she goes or not her children are
well. Almira got cold by going to the fair her throat had

92

ben sore three days the seats damp. if you wold write and let me know what day you could come to meet us or when would be the most convenient time and if you apoint a day then it will clear me from the charge of being in a great hury for I want to come home. I dont want to stay here all winter and I know that I could be useful thar I dreamd last night I got a letter from you but wakd up before I read it. if this reaches you by saterday Mail write a sunday and say when I shall come home. thare was a funeral every day for a week and two a day last saterday and sunday. Jo Bahneys [Massillon cabinet maker & coffin maker] has two hearses and they ware both kept going. if you see my sanktimonious sister [Susan Jackson Wright] before I get home tell her to have her lecture ready for I will be disapointed if she fails to give me a curtain lecture. I was at a duch [dutch] ball in the Madisson Hall but dont tell her that for I want to get out of that as easy as posible in fact I dont know how I got in to it. they are starting up the furnace again now write soon and tell constance [young granddaughter] I am coming home I have some visiting to doo yet. I have ben reading John Brown don't get out of patience with my noncence and if I can find a clear spot on your face I will kiss you when I come home   *your Mother*

      M Hardgrove

On board the Campion
Nov.18 '62
Mr. William Hardgrove

Dear Brother. as we will soon be into Memphis where we can mail our letters I would write you a few lines to keep you posted of our whereabouts. We will get into Memphis tonight some time if we have good luck. I wrote mother a letter after we left St. genevieve which I mailed at Cairo.

The next day after I wrote we run on to a bar in the river and did not get off for 24 hours. We got into Cairo yesterday morning. we passed Columbus yesterday afternoon.

We tied up last just above a large bar in the river.

This morning the regiment and horse got off and marched down below the bar. I remained on board while we went over. The boat rubed very hard on one place going over. We passed island No. 10 this morning, it dont look like a hard place to take. It is low island We also passed the reck of our old transport, the Universe, which took us up the Tennessee river from Paris Landing to Pittsburg Landing. we passed Fort Pillow this afternoon. It is a hard looking place. It looks as if there had been some fighting done there. One large siege gun is blown up. I still have the ague. It has changed from the night to the forenoon and a very hapy change it is for I can now sleep at night.

94

I am entirely straped no money. It cost me more to come back than I expected. My trip home and back cost me $60. When we go into camp I want you to send me ten dollars As soon as we land I will write to you here to send it.

If my resignation is acceped it will be two or three weeks before I can hear from it or may be be longer

I have not heard from home since I left.

Your brother
Lieut. J. H. Hardgrove

Mitchell H. Hardgrove[32]
b. May 26, 1838
d. Oct. 22, 1862
in defense of his
country
at St. Louis
Age 24 yrs. 4 mo. 27 days
Vet: Co. I, 76th Regiment
L.O.T.I.

Camp Steele Mississippi
December 11, '62
Mr. William Hardgrove
Dear Brother: I received your very welcome letter this
evening with ten dollars and the postage stamps which
came in might good play. I have been out of money ever
since we have been here.

There has been no chance to borrow any as the
whole regt. is about as hard up as I was . It is very ruff
living here without money.

I received a letter this week from mother and
Minerva. I am looking for my papers every day and as soon
as they come I will brake for home. Tomorrow the Major
will be here with recruits for the regt. and he will have a
commission for me as 1st Lieut. of Co. B. I will not not
except it and that will end that little trouble.

I am beginning to feel much better but I have not
got the ague rooted out yet.

So you are going to try teaching again It will not
take very hard studying to go through as they are not very
far advanced, and a small school. There is nothing new of
importance in camp. Soldiers still come into camp from up
the river.

Our forces are swelling up very fast. We must have
near fourty thousand men here on boath sides of the river.

The expedition that went down the river some time ago came back last sunday They went across to the railroad that runs to Jackson and injured it some, got chased by guerrillas lost a gun and came home. On our side cotton is coming in pritty freely. One man in the last twenty four hours has brought in twenty four bales which is worth six thousand dollars. The speculation is a big one. Our boys are building log shanties and preparing for winter. Nothing more.

> *Your Brother*
> *Lieut. J. H. Hardgrove*

Henry Comes Home

Lieutenant John Henry Hardgrove made it home! And just a few days after Christmas! While he was still in time to enjoy the gaiety of the holidays with his sisters and families, his mother was wintering with son William and family in Mt. Vernon, Ohio. In the early weeks at home, however, Henry's thoughts still wandered back to what the men in his regiment were doing. When Margaret returned to Massillon then, in late spring, the bustle of life resumed with extreme enthusiasm for the most part. The exceptions were soldiers' military funerals that she and family attended at the Methodist church in Massillon.

Massillon Ohio
Jan. 5 '63
Mrs. Margaret Hardgrove

Dear Mother:

>*I got back from the land of Dixsee a week ago last saturday night.*

>*I am well and rest of the folks here.*

>*If I get my clothes done I will be out to see you the last of the week.*

>*We had a big dance here last week. Hiram Bahney and all the family were here. Last saturday I was out hunting and shot two rabits and two squirrels.*

>*Our regiment was going on board the boats when I lef for Vicksburg.*

>>>>*Your son*

>>>*J. H. Hardgrove*

Massillon March 1863 Miss Margaret Hardgrove

Dear Margaret I just receive your letter and hasten to answer I was glad to get your letter as I wanted to hear from home I got one from Minerva [and] from Ann [daughter Ann] today and as Minerva was not here I opend it. she has gone out to berlin [Berlin, Ohio] to see Ada she went on the cars to frederick [Fredericksburg] would hire a conveyance to Midletown [Middletown]. Hariet is as well as usual. Mary Mac has been at Archers ever since I come. her and Almira were down here once. Mary Archer was here all the afternoon. a fryday and a saterday night she

come down with the men in the waggon they waited for the
ten oclock train to come to get the papers and Mary staid
here. Delia May [possibly boarder] was here when I come
but Hariet told her she could not keep her so she went to
benetts [probably another Hardgrove cousin] and pays
three dollars per week for boarding she had plenty of mony.
last week thare was 3 dead soldiers brot home from
Murfreesboro [Battle of Stones River in Central Tennessee]
and buried. the people met at the Methodist church thare
was a sermon preached. all the soldiers about town went in
prosession they was buried with the honors of war. they had
marshal musick and fired guns over the graves. one was a
son of austin alens [possibly Allen] ones name was Who
[Hugh?] whitaker. they ware all wounded at that fight. we
have no family but Hariet Hiram and my self and George.
Minerva got a new dress and made it before she went away
she intended to go to Midletown with the Mail Carier and
hiram went down see him and he carid the Mail on horse
back so he orderd the omnibus to come up and she went on
the cars. she will stay a few weeks a visiting among the old
Neighbours. they have examination at the union school this
week. thare has ben a great prominading on the street every
day. I have not been up at Archers since last monday week.
Orrick and Henry [possibly Archer family boarder] was

down here a sundy evening I dont think thare is much prospect of your geting a new aunt soon. Minervas old beau J C cald here the day after she went away and inquired for her and hiram got a card of invitation for him and Hariet and Minerva to a surprise dance at george Russels but she was not here and neither him or Hariet went. I was sorry to hear that your papa did not get his boy. george [Harriet's little boy] can say anything we tel him. he begins to talk right well. when you write again let me hear how aunt is geting along and what they heard from Henry. we have had a good quiet time. thare is not so many coming in as thare used to. Hiram has been engaged reading a book the secrets of the west he reads every night till bed time and I read in day time so we have both got through. write to me often as you can and I will answer

your grandMother

M Hardgrove

Massillon   April 20th 63
Dear Ann I promisd to write again soon. Minerva got back from homes co [Holmes County] last fryday she hapend to have the company of Mrs. Perkey from here to Midletown

they stayd all night at Fredrick [Fredricksburg]at firestones

he is Mrs.perkeys unkle he took them over to the widow

perkeys. Minerva stayed thare one night and the next

morning sidney and her rode a horse back over to Ed

perkeys. she stayd with Milly from thursday till monday and

ed took her to berlin [Berlin, Ohio] she stayd thare nearly

three weeks curtis fechd her and Mary Downs to Midletown

they both went to see salina stayd all night with her. Henry

[probably salina's husband] was away working at his

trade. they live not far from old Henry Pownds. they went

to old Isaac pounds and Mary Ann insulted them they was

talking about the war. Mary Downs tryd to enlighten her

but you might as well talk to a monkey. they never invited

them in to see the old man he was in bed they stayd in the

kitchen. old brother Pangburn died the week before last.

Mary [Archer] has been poorly with the liver disease and

so have I but she got a good bach of dandaline and we are

using it. old Mrs. Claper sally Hardgroves Mother come up

yesterday morning and went with me to church after

meeting I went home with her and took diner. Hariet and

Hiram had went out to Billy Bahneys and I come home. I

went down to joes and eat my super. orrick and Henry

[Henry is now at home] come in the evening. now I dont

know whether Henry got that receipt yet or not I wont ask

him nor he wont tell me with out he showed me a letter he got from Wm. but I did not ask him if he had sent it or if intended to. he got the forefinger and midle finger on his left hand tore all to pieces nearly last week he will not be able to work for some time the first joint of the midle finger was seperated but Mary doctors it and of course its well done. Henry is galanting Cordelia Razor old ben Razors Daughter I dont think he has any notion of Marying or orrick either. but O J goes it regular. if orrick could save enough of mony to start to house keeping with he would but he has to pay Mary Shaffer [Shaefer] more for keeping his boy [John Richard] than would keep a family he has Richard working in the shop with him. he boards at Archers. Mary [Archer] has a big family to cook for they have eleven in family they have a hired hand working on farm. Wright mire is dead. he died in the Hospital. he was a drafted soldier his wife is in deep trouble. he died at Mempohis and another Neighbor Jacob Brakebill. Hariet was eating her breakfast this morning and hurt her tooth so she jumpt and hollowed and was nearly crazy all the forenoon this afternoon she went to the dentist and got four teeth extracted. a saterday Hariet and me went up to Marys we left Minerva here to get diner and she come up after diner and brot georgey [Harriet's little boy]. Minerva come down yesterday evening and pichd in to the work today and then went back to Marys this evening. wright soon and let me know if Henry has sent that receipt

your Mother   M Hardgrove

Copperhead Demonstrations

It was the month of May in Massillon, but the whole village attended local churches for special Thanksgiving Day services. Henry and cousin O. J. had their sights set on a couple of local girls. One Saturday night, the brass band wagon pulled by 4 horses "serenaded" all over town. Meanwhile, people also filled the streets to hear Col. Anderson make a speech from the upper porch of the American House Hotel. Henry had just applied for a situation in the invalid corps, and Canton, Ohio was bracing for an ox roast and a "venomous" copperhead demonstration.

Massillon   May 9th 63   Miss Margaret A Hardgrove

Dear Maggy I receive your letter dated the 5th and 28th of April and take the present opertunity to answer it I have had a bad cold and sore throat for two or three weeks. I have been using flax seed tea I think my throat is a little beter today. last thursday was thanksgiving day or rather fast day and every boddy went to church thar was four churches united and had preaching in the prisbyterian church the Methodist prisbyterian episcopal and reformed Lutheran. the house is large and was very full I was at church in the fore noon and at night. the four preachers sat side of each other it looked kind of sociable. they prayd for the soldiers for the president and all the officers of our government the Methodist preacher is an educated smart man has great comand of language. yesterday I atended church at our own church and Hariet and I went to the episcopalion at night I can go to church twice a day here. Last week thare was a panarama and a saterday night Dolly Dutten concert. to night the panarama is showd again. a saterday night the brass band waggon with four horses and a full band of Musick was sernading all over town. O J has quit Archers and boards here with hariet. she has a hired girl. Minerva is with Mary. hariet and her girl is cleaning house today upstairs and papering a room

Henrys fingers are geting beter but it will be a long time before the midle finger gets well he comes down to town evey day. I see in the Dayly comershal that the uniontown [possibly Uniontown, Pennsylvania] folks have been very much alarmd. thare four

106

thousand Rebel Cavelry had come to Morgantown [West Virginia] and took posesion of the town and they hoisted the Rebel flag on the court House. the men all skedadled and left the women and children to fight the Rebles. I will send the paper if they go down to uniontown [probably Uniontown, Pennsylvania]. Jim Mclean [friend in Brownsville, Pennsylvania] and gen. Beeson will not think hard to devide what they have I supose with the sesesh. I wonder if gen Beeson would plead up southern rights if they take his horses and catle and all his corn hay and oats. george [Archer] says if you know of any body that want to hire send them to him he wants a hand he has one but he is worth nothing. Ruth Earl, Mary Shaffer [Shaefer] and betsey [Hardgrove of Butterbridge] was here today. orrick had Dickey [his young son] helping him in the shop two weeks. george [possibly cousin George Earl also home from Civil War] and Henry and orrick was going to get thare pickture all on one plate to send to Aunt susan [Margaret's sister]. orrick come down before they did and when Henry [John Henry] and george come they couldent find him so george and Henry got thares and george says if they can ever make the connection they will have them all together and send them to Aunt. Hiram takes the Dayly com [Daily Commercial, ad paper] and I have a paper to read every night

write soon   M Hardgrove [grandmother]

Massillon   May 10th 63   [Ann is daughter-in-law Judith Ann]
Dear Ann I have a few minites this monday afternoon as luly
[unknown person] has took georgey down street. Hariet and the girl
are cleaning house. they was at it all last week and will have two
days more before they are through they paperd two rooms upstairs
and took up all the carpit and cleaning the woodwork. thare is a
great excitement here about the late batles and yesterday morning a
dispach come that Richmond was taken and this morning another
dispach that the rebels had got posession again. every kind of
business is going on here as lively as if thare was no war. I believe it
was saterday evening the word come that Richmond was taken and
the boys had bonfires in the streets the band was out sernading till
12 or 1 oclock. Henry has gone to work again through his fingers are
not well. Henry sticks to his Razor girl and orrick to his Dutch gal
but I dont think they have any intention to Marry. Mary and Minerva
was here a saterday Minerva went out home with Laura Bahney.
yesterday her and laura went to Richville [small community south of
Massillon] to meeting. Rachel everharts husband preachd. he is an
old man and all right preacher. I went to deciple church and Hariet
came and brot georgey [Harriet's little boy] he is so rude I dont want
her to take him again. he will talk out in meeting. I got my bonet
done up Mrs Falk alterd it. I got a new dress fifty cents a yard its not
made yet. I will send you a piece of it when its cut out it cost me six
dollars. Mary and her little girls went out to church the other side of
Deans yesterday. well now it is bed time and Hariet and I

have just come in. we started down street at dusk to get a glass of ale
and here we found a five or six hundred standing in the street
listening to col. Manderson [possibly Col. Anderson] making a
speech from the uper porch of the American house we stood thare til
we got tired and then went in to the grosery and got a glass of the
best ale I ever drank and as we came up thare was about a regement
of boys burning barels in the street. george was asleep and the girl
staid with him. I see by todays paper it was all humbug about our
folks taking Richmond I will send Wm a paper with col. Andersons
speech if he has not had it. I want him to read it. I went home with
Minerva yesterday evening and staid all night and this morning her
and me went and hunted a mess of dock greens and I brot them
home and I walkd up to kendal [Kendal was a community on east
edge of Massillon] and brot a gallon of soap for the girl to clean the
house with and I am tired for I have been on my feet all day. george
[Harriet's little boy] can talk right well. I cannot write half what I
want to. it is late orrick has just come in the band is playing and the
street is crowd with folks going home write soon

M Hardgrove

Massillon   June 29th   63
Dear Margaret as this is sunday evening and I have been alone I
think I must write to you. I went to church in the fore noon come

home and helpd Hariet get diner. Henry and orrick Hiram and Laura was here for diner. Hariet and georgey went home with Laura. orrick went up to earls [cousin George Earl] and Hiram went to the depot. Henry went up to bed to take a snoose. the girl had gone home. she has come now and is geting super and Henry has come home. I went up to Marys last wednesday. a fryday her and me come down to town she fetchd the two little girls [Mary's and George's *littlest* daughters Delia and Amelia] to get thare pictures taken. I went back with her to get my super. Henry had killd nine squirls and Minerva cookd them for super. yesterday Minerva come down with me. her and Hariet went down street and after dark Minerva and I went down to the confectionarys [Pietzekerr's] and got some ice cream thare ware three ladies come in while we was eating ours and got each a plate full of ice cream. I got a letter from your papa last week but thare was not—this is monday morning—enough in it to satisfy me. I wanted to hear more. the methodist preacher give them a union sermon yesterday evening. I had quit writing and took a walk down street I met Minerva and we ware coming home and we met Henry, george earl and orrick going to church. they wanted me to go with them but I thought it would be too warm and did not go but I wish I had went for the boys says they never heard a beter discourse. it was not a sermon it was a union speach. I have just got a letter from Ruth [sister-in-law near Mt. Vernon] she says she had a letter from george Lerner in May. he was at Miligans bend. he was living and well at that time. Henry has made aplication for a situation in the invalid corp. if he gets it he will be imployd in the garison duty and have the same office he had before. they are going to have a big time at canton [Canton, Ohio] a saterday but all the men on the muster Roll will have too parade here and be organisd. the folks are going to have an ox roasted whole. the coperheads are going to have a demonstration and I expect if a union man hapens to jostle a coperhead in passing him they will kick up a fuss. they are so venomous. it seems as if the evil one has possision of them I would not like to go. though I would like to hear the speakers. thare is to be some half dozen Honerables thare. Ruth wants to know if we have any locusts here. she says they keep squallng constantly all the time. thares not many in town but out at Marys thare is plenty. now Margaret I want you to write me a long letter and tell me all about constance and eves baby and if you had any strawburys or rasburys how Mrs. Lu frasher is and Aunts family and how your Mothers Health is this summer and curtis and your papa and how many chickens you have. george [Hariet's little boy] is a bully boy he can talk anything. Minerva got a letter from Ada a few days ago give my love to all the family your grandMother   M Hardgrove

O J's Invention on Public Exhibit

Until twilight crept in to dim her writing paper, Margaret penned news to her Mt. Vernon family to update them on serious current events, always so much to tell. Mary Archer was heavily involved in practicing her homeopathic expertise, which usually saw excellent results on both horse and man. There was also an epidemic of whooping cough hitting local children especially hard, with 2 or 3 funerals a day. In late September, more disturbing mass meetings were held in Massillon, and Margaret noted she barely resisted voicing her own public rebuttal aimed at the main speaker about lies he was spewing. Meanwhile, the Massillon fair was providing entertainment and release of stresses of the day. And O. J. Hardgrove was striving for last-minute perfection of his agricultural invention—the horse rake —to put on public exhibit.

Massillon   August 31st   63   Mrs. J A Hardgrove

Dear Ann I have a few minits idle this evening and I thought I would write. I got a letter from Clara Halsted and have just answerd it. a saterday night I went to the madison Hall to hear profesor McCoy from washington he is calld one of the greatest orators of the time he was a fine looking man and had as much theatrical jesture as any person could desire. the house was crowded jam full. those that could not get seats stood up and many could not get in at all. for the last week I have done little. I came up here yesterday to go with george and Mary to go to earls [Ruth and Gill Earl] and just as we were going to start a man come and brot georges [Archer] colt from the pasture it had something like the quinsey it was the pony mares colt two years old last spring. it could hardly breathe its throat was swelld. Mary went to work boild hops and vinagar bathd it and put on a poultice. they sent for orrick and she tended it all night. george and her went to the barn with hot vinagar today it is beter it was a great pet. capt. Briggs has come home he and his wife are to be here tomoro. orrick Martin is to be here this evening. george [Archer] has bought a cider Mill a hand mill they made some cider they have plenty of good eating aples and pears. Henry has give up going to the Army. I got my bureau up from the depot a wednesday. orrik sent it up on a dray the freight was only 25 cents and I had to pay the drayman fifteen cents. hariet has a very good girl she pays her a dollar and a quarter. thare is a great many children dying. peter [unknown] made six small coffins in three days last week. thare has been several grown people died too. thare was two or three funerals a day last week. yesterday a returned soldier was buried he had only ben at home a few days. it is geting so late I cant see to write up here without a candle. I must close. Minerva and almira [Mary Archer's teen step-daughter] has got new dresses they got new gingham dreses while I was out at your house. and now they got something else I don't know what it is. write soon. litle george [Bahney's son] has not been well he had a direa and a fever the whooping cough is in town. last night orrick come up her after night with liddy Archer she had been to New Philadelphia. he drank six glasses of cider and went back to town to set up with a dead man. thare is a great many dying every day. thare is a funeral some days two or three. orrick said Hariet was sick in bed yesterday all day. I am going down this morning. we have had a litle rain george [Archer] will get no clover seed they will be no pickles here the cucumbers vines are all dead and very few tomatoes. tell Aunt susey Clara Halstead wants her to write to her. I have no time to write any more now. Liddy Archer is going to town and I must go down and see how Hariet and litle george is write your Mother

M Hardgrove

I will send you a piece of the girls dresses the green is Minervas and the biaze Almiras

Massillon   Oct 2nd 63   Mr. Wm Hardgrove

Dear son there has been so much going on to draw crouds of people here so much excitement noise and confusion that it is hard to get time to write but I think I must write to you. we have had two big Mass meetings last thursday week the union people had thare meeting and a monday they withdraw your army. folks had thares and one would have thought that all germany had been pourd out. they come from three or 4 countys. the most vulgar and visious rable there was a great many union people thare. I got in hearing distance of the speaker Dan vorhies [Rep. Daniel W. Voorhees] of indiana. he said the abolitions and the republicans wanted a new bible a new god and a new world. I could hardly help teling him he lied and he knew it. well since I wrote the above I took litle georgey and went up to Archers. I staid all night and about nine oclock in come Henry. it was very stormy and raining. before he got one step from the dorre he was surounded. everyone in the house had him by the hand or leg or any plase thy could get holt of him orrick was thare and Will Archer and his comrade charley bobah pronounced bobaw. such rejoicing and such a noise you never seen. Will Archer and his comrade had come a wednesday. they came from Milwaka whare all Henry had been. I will leave him to tell the story himself. he had traveld a great distance since he left home. george had been in a great deal of trouble about Will. and I was about Henry. for I did not know whare he was. but a saterday night the boys were all thare and we all felt glad. Will and his comrade are going on to old philadephia. I come down to town in the evening and I left orrick thare and him and Henry come down after dark. Henry staid here last night he went up to Archers this morning. the fair come of last week thare was a great many people thare but very little to look at. the floral hall had but litle in it. Rusels had a good deal of thare mesheenery thare and orrick had a horse rake. he had got it up on a new plan. he had been working at it nearly two weeks. it has long crooked iron teath. I cant discribe it satisfactoryly. the shows and flying horses and grossserys done a good business thare was very litle horse racing and but litle stock thare. I got a letter form Clara Halsted she wants me to send her a copy of her Mothers picture I had wrote to her that I had a picture. I cant get it til a wedensday. Hariet has been aflicted with biles to that she could hardly be out of bed. she is not over them yet. I want you to write soon and let me know how your flax seed turnd out and clover seed and how you are making out with your cider press. georges colts all had the quinsy or something like it. he has three one [probably one year old] yearling and two two years-old. I wont to know whare Lucinda is now and how Aunt susans family is your Mother

    M Hardgrove

Massillon Ohio
Oct 18   '63
Mr. Wm. Hardgrove
Dear Brother I will try and send you a few lines today to keep you
posted of my whereabouts:

I got back a few days ago from the long tramp. I went from
here to Cincinnati and there I got in with a watch establishment and
invested a hundred dollars in composition waches. I got them very
cheap for $50 a doz I went from there to Columbus, Pittsburg,
Harrisburg, Lancaster, Philadelphia and Baltimore and from there
to Washington and from there I went down to the Army of the
Potomac. I went as far as the Culpeper Court House. the 5th army
corps was just paid off when I went down there and I soon sold the
remainder of my watches to a very good advantage and returned
home.

I would have went bace again with a n other lot but I didn't
like to run the risk of being gobbled up by Mr. Secesh for the army
was preparing for a grand Skedaddle toward Washington. And I see
that I just got away in time for they have commenced the skedaddle.
Old Virginia is a hard looking country. you cannot tell what it did
originally look like it is so cut up by the Army. There is only here
and there a poor family living. those that were able have all left.

Culpeper Court House where I was is about 60 miles from
Alexandra and ten miles from the Rapidan. It is about the size of
Millersburg [Millersburg, Ohio].

*I am going to start with Georges Patent Hounds next
wednesday for dayton [Dayton, Ohio] and Hamilton [Hamilton Co.,
Ohio] and likely further owning to what success I have.*

Your Brother
J. H. Hardgrove

*We are all well. I will write to you again from Dayton or Hamilton.
We went Union big here over 200 in Perry [a Massillon township].*

Massillon Ohio

Dec. 12 1863
Mr. William Hardgrove
*Dear Brother, I thought I would write you a few lines this morning
but paper is a little too scarce for me to write much and it is a little
too muddy for me to go to town for more. It has been raining and
sleeting here for the last twenty four hours.*

*It is a good day to read Old Abes Message and
Procclamation.*

*I got back from the West a few days and I intend to go back
soon I went on to Detroit Mich. where I got through with the Hounds
and Fifth Wheel and went up into the norther part of the State
traping I did well at it and I am going back soon I have made
enough money in the last six month to pay off the 250 I owed on my
house and have a hundred left*

George and I are going into the bending business next summer I am going up to Bucyrus to buy a lot for the business. We went to get the old shop that stands at the top of the stone Brige.

It is a mighty good Business but it will take all the capital we can raise to start it.

I am going out to see you this winter some time I think.

Mother is here and all right.

The folks around here are beginning to feel quite shiftless about the Draft. I have sent to Washington for my papers.

Last fall when I made application for a position in the Invalid Corps the District surgeon gave me a certificate saying I was not subject to the Draft and unfit for field service. If I can get them from Washington I believe they will clear me

> *Your Brother*
> *J. H. Hardgrove*

Mock Battles on Massillon Streets

Great news in February of 1864: "Orrick is married at last!" And so an otherwise cold, drab season took on a holiday atmosphere within his family circle. Afterward, Margaret had wintered with Mary's family as Harriet and Hiram awaited the birth of another child. All these events eventually found Margaret so under the weather (doctoring with her sasperilla) that she did not even have energy enough to write to _anyone_. Ah, but finally one blustery day she rallied to pen a letter to her daughter-in-law, "Ann," near Mt. Vernon, telling about the wedding. As spring approached, soldiers were having mock battles in the streets of Massillon, and Margaret occupied herself by keeping tabs on all of her grandchildren—especially Harriet's little boy, George, who was "enough to set anyboddy crazy."

Massillon   Feb 16th 64   Mrs. J A Hardgrove
Dear Ann I came down to town yesterday morning and I
thought I would write to day and tell you how the weding
went off. orrick is maried at last. Archer, Henry, george
Earl and little Ruth [Orrick's young daughter]went with
him over to canton. They went on the cars they were maried
and after taking some refreshment came back on the one
oclock train. they come to Archers and Mary had a big
super ready for them. Mrs. Anderson and her husband,
Isaac Doxey, JohnWarwick ware thare. a fryday they come
to Hariets. on a saterday they went up to Mary shaffers
[Shaefer]. yesterday evening they all went to earls [Ruth
and Gill Earl]. Hariet and Hiram and me staid at home.
orrick and his wife, Minerva and laura Bahney all went in
a two seated cariage and took little george along. this is a
very blustering storm day. I have not been very well. I have
a sore toe it criples me so I cant wear a shoe. Henry come
with me to town yesterday and got me a pair of ruber shoes.
Mary and george and Henry was at earls [Ruth and Gill]
last night. I presume you would like to know what sort of a
woman the bride is. she is small about the size of selina
Hall very quiet very pios [pious] and I think very firm and I
believe she will be a good Housekeeper and very
equanomical. she dresses plain wares but lite triming she is

29 years old. I have great hope she will bring orrick in to her rules. reform him. she is a member of the presbyterian church. Hariet has very poor health ever since she was confined. she looks miserable but is able to go about and litle Will [Harriet's baby] is as fat as a pig. Hariet has had chills and fever once every ten days or two weeks her liver is out of order. I have been up to Marys most of the time since new year. I have it very comfortable thare and here I have the care of the children and george is enough to set any boddy crazy. Willie is a very good quiet babe. laura Bahney has been to canton for a week she come back yesterday and Minerva took her out home today and it is so cold and snowy she has just got back nearly froze. she brot some butter a pail of crout some aples some dried corn and some onions. Mrs. linns [Linn] little girl is dead. her only child. I don't know what is the reason none of you writes to me I have ben looking till I am tired and no letter. I wrote some time ago to know if thare would be any chance of geting home made carpit in that county. orrick and hariet both wants some. I asked Henry yesterday morning if he would go out to your house with me in the spring. oh yes he would. but he talks of going to boating [unclear if word is correct to her meaning] in the spring. boating oar for the furnace. I wish you would write soon I have not writen a

letter this winter to any body but you. I got a very nice ring
for a birthday present. Henry got it. Hariet sent for me to
come down here the ninth to take diner and she had no
great shakes of a diner after all. she had some cand
peaches. they have a fashion of stuffing turkeys and
*chickens with oysters and I dont like it your Mothe*r
Margaret Hardgrove

Massillon   March 6th 64 Miss Margaret A Hardgrove
Dear Maggy I had come to the conclusion that you had all
forgotten me I had writen three times and waited and
wachd for a reply but got none till the 24 of febuary. I
received a letter from your Mother dated the 18 of January
it had not come here till the day I got it. orrick got a letter
from your papa a day or two before I got your Mothers. so
you had lucinda [Lucinda who had previously been staying
in Massillon to attend school] to go to school with you this
winter. lucinda Hardgrove was sick when your Mother
write. I want you to write soon and let me know how she is
and how Ann gets along with lucinda. if she could not
govern her when she was younger I am afraid she will not
be able to controll her now. she seems distiend to be a
trouble to her friends. thare is a great many soldiers here

123

thursday they had a sham batle in the street and the citizens gave them a festaval or rather a super a fryday. they had thare entertainment at canton. Hariet and sharlott sterling went to canton to buy carpet they can get capet beter and cheaper thare. they went on the ten oclock train. Henry come here before diner and Hiram and him went on the 3 oclock train. Hiram took george along they come home on the 7 oclock train. george can go a head of any boy of his size for noise and mischief I have ever come across. he calls me branma and when he gets mad at me he calls me a brat or any boddy that afronts him he calls them brat. Minerva and Almira got new silk dresses. sharlot is making Minervas a dollar and a half per yard. Minerva got a new blue deliane. I will send you a piece. I got a black Alapaca it is seventy cents. cost me eight dollars and 25 cents. I would like to come out to see you all again in the spring but I dont know how it turn out. Almira is going to sharlot sterling to learn to make dresses when the spring work commences and Minerva will stay with Mary this sumer. she is going to get a new bonet when the new goods come in the spring. I have been using the sassaperilla [bark of root of sassafras tree used in medicines and tea] and yellow dock all winter and I think my health is much better than it was. orrick got a large botle full in the begining of the winter and he only used a few times out of it and george Archer got a botle and took a few teaspoons full and Mary and I used the rest of it and then Henry got a botle of the sassperila without the yellow dock so I have had it very convenient as I am a few days here and a few days thare I have medicine all the time. george [Archer] laughs at me he says I take any thing thats calld medacine. after I come home from church today Minerva went up to Marys. Mrs. Joe Baney [Hiram's sister-in-law] has a young son born last tuesday. she has nurse to wait on her at five dollars a week. her babe isnt as pretty as our little Willie. our little Will is as white as babys gets and as fat. he is so quiet and good. Hariet and sharlot come up to Mary last wednesday and brot george and Wilie. Mrs. Wilson and Issac Archers and his wife and his brother and two Nephews the name of Buraway was all thare for super and george sent them down in the waggon in the evening. Henry Archer is a soldier. has re-enlisted and is home on furlough. I come down a thursday with Mary and the children [little Delia and baby Amelia] in the waggon and I am here yet but tomorrow I am going up agin write to me soon. I will try Henry to come out with me this spring when the roads is good your grandMother

M Hardgrove

Massillon Independent

Spring was in the air, and Margaret was sending her granddaughter Maggy some humorous bits out of the "independent," the new Massillon newspaper. Almira was learning the dressmaking trade with sharlot sterling, Mary attended the Jake Hersheys farm sale in Lawrence Township and bought a big wheel to spin stocking wool from her own sheep and Orrick was bringing his young son Dick to work with him in the shop. Meanwhile, there were a great many soldiers getting married while at home on furlough.

Massillon monday March 29th (1864) Miss Margaret Hardgrove Dear Maggy I think I must write to you today and send you a paper thare is nothing in the dayly com [weekly advertising paper] that is interesting so I will send you some independents [Massillon Independent]. you may find something to laugh at in them maybe. orrick has been at work. ever since he was maried he goes to canton every saterday evening. his wife is sick now. they sent him a dispach that she was worse and he went over on the 3 oclock train. he come back this morning he says she has a beeling in her ear and has the intermiting feever. they ware going to move this week but I am afraid she wont be able. I am anxious to see them a housekeeping. Aunt susan talks of coming in to see us and fech Lucinda. I wish you could come along if she comes. I will go home with her. yesterday was such a lovely pleasant day you know it was easter sunday. I went up to Marys last tuesday and a fryday evening Mary sent the boy down for Hariet and the children. she staid till yesterday. Minerva come up a saterday evening and yesterday morning the boys brot us all down in the wagon. Mary and her two little girls went with me to church. Hariet has such a lame back she cant stand straight. Almira [Mary's teen stepdaughter] is learning the dress making with sharlot sterling. she boards at home. she goes down at nine in the morning and quits at four in the evening. she takes some cakes in and eats with them. Almira is a fast sewer and good sewer but she is a ratle brained girl. Archer [son-in-law George] has been afflicted *with the rheumatic pains in his legs so he can hardly sleep at night. Mary will get her garden plowed in this spring. I think she will find room for steady work all sumer. she bought a big wheel at Jake Hersheys sale. she is going to get her wool carded and spin her own stocking wool. they have two sheep of thare own and eight on shares. Jake hershey is going to leave today or tomorrow for Illanoise. Liza and husband bought his place at $5000. they had a big exabition at the stone school house last saterday evening. orrick had brot Dick [Orrick's young son] here to work in the shop with him and Dick went up home a saterday to go to the exabition and he has not come back yet. thare was a great many solders got Maried while they ware at home on furlough but they are nearly all gone back now. when you see Aunt susan tell her to come as soon as she can or Mary will get tired waiting for her. she says she has looked for her so often and been disapointed. I hope she wont disapoint her this time. tell your Mother to let you come along but if you would come in June when the flowers are in bloom it would be pleasanter. I dont know whether I sent you a piece of Minervas last new dress. I will put a scrap in this. I have just wrote a letter to sarah Huston. write soon and dont forget to tell constance [little daughter of son William in Mt. Vernon] I will come and see her soon your grandMother   Margaret*

Massillon   Apr 20th 64   Mrs. J A Hardgrove [Wm.'s wife]
Dear Ann I received your leter a monday evening and I was very
sorry to hear your whole family has been so much aflicted I have not
been well myself for two weeks. you know every spring my health
fails but I hope I will feel better in a week or two. I had been talking
to Henry about going out to your house the morning before I got
your letter and he said he would go about the 19th of May. I was at
Archers in the morning and in the evening I was coming down to
town I met Minerva going up to Marys and she had your letter and I
asked Henry that evening when we would go. he said about the 15th
but he is gone. the lord knows where or when he will come back so if
I am well enough and no preventing provedence I will come about
the 15th of may if I am able to come sooner I will write to you as I
hope to see you soon. I will not write much more now. we have so
much to doo today. Minerva is going to stay with Mary this sumer.
Almira [Mary's stepdaughter] is learning the dress making with
sterling girl. orrick has got to house keeping. I wrote to Ruth twice
but she never answerd my leter. I am sorry to hear the measels and
small pox are in your neighborhood. if the wet wether was over I
think I would feel beter. Hariet has better health now than she had.
well I must quit and run down to the post office with this in time for
it to go to day that it may reach you by saterday. this is thursday..
Hariet is going to mop the room whare I am writing and I must quit.
I will fetch the daisies your Mother   M Hardgrove

Massillon   May 5th 1864   Mr Wm Hardgrove

Dear son I wrote to you last week I believe that I would come out to
see you the 15 of May but I find that will be on sunday so I will come
on saterday the 19. Henry was gone away when I wrote but he was
only gone one week. he is here now but whether he will go with me
or not I dont know. my health is so poor that I am not able to travel
now but if the weather becomes setled again I think on. this is a
beautiful morning and I hope we will have a litle pleasant weather
once more. every bodys daisies froze last winter so I dont know if I
can get any. Henry says he will go with me but I dont take his word
for he will say yes to any thing I ask him. Henry is waiting

M Hardgrove

Buggy Ride on Butterbridge

Granddaughter Maggie finally came to visit in the summer of 1864. And days of August opened into wonderful jaunts for Margaret with her daughters while their husbands were busy elsewhere. She and Mary took a buggy ride back to Butterbridge Road where she and husband John and the kids used to live near the Hardgrove homestead. Then one warm evening she and Harriet strolled up to the village for ice cream. Meanwhile, Minerva and Almira were invited to Orrick's home for the day. The following week, unfortunately, O J's mare jumped onto the car track and was nearly killed.

Massillon   August 7th '64   Miss Margaret Hardgrove

Dear Maggy I thought I would take the present oportunity to write a
few lines to you. Mary sent joe down with the buggy for Hariet and
me this morning early and we came up here for breakfast. george
Archer, charly, Almira and Minerva all went to franklin they started
yesterday morning about four oclock in georges new carriage. Mr.
sutherd went with them. a fryday Mary and me was to earls [Ruth
Earl]. I come home with her and yesterday her and the little girls
[Mary's and George's little daughters Almira and Delia] and me
went down to town thare was a show in town and we went down and
saw the man walk the rope he walked up and then backward down.
then he sit down on the rope and swung by his hands then by his
foot. he danced and turned sumersets. Mary has old Dolly and the
buggy to go when she pleases and her and I have been visiting. we
went to Robisons one day and we went up to george Hardgroves. we
went to old Bahneys. Minerva has staid here at Marys ever since
you was here. Hiram is working at canton. he gets better wages
there. Hariot and I have good times we can cook and eat when we
please. we dont have to go by the whisle. we have had a long
Drough every thing was parchd up but last tuesday we had a good
rain. hariets sistern is nearly half full her cucumber vines is full of
cucumbers yesterday thare sprinkle. Hariet and I went down a
monday evening to pitscars [Pietzcker's Massillon confectionary
shop] to get some ice cream we took george and Willie along. we eat

our ice cream and had to hury home the rain was coming on. she took Willie out of the buggy and put georgey in and we got home just as it began to rain we had to run. Minerva and Almira got new calico dresses alike. Almira made hers last week and they wore them up to franklin they took tatharo silk dresses along. Almira is bound to have her things that girl took. they will not be home before tuesday as they went to go into the cinhaga falls tomorow. last tuesday Minerva and Almira spent the day at orricks. avas sister was there and had invited them to come. orricks three hundred dollar mare got nearly killd yesterday she jumped out of Rusels lot and went on the Rail Road and got knockt off by the cars. he told me last night that it had been fifty dollar bills. I dont expect she will ever be worth anything if she does live. we have heard nothing from Will Archer or Mike since they left. we had two young chickens for breakfast. tell Henry [that] Norman steffy is killed. he was a fine looking young man. his Mother a widow and him her only son. he was an officer. I dont know what office. tell susan [Margaret's sister]to write. I want to hear from her and what news from the boys in the Army. my health has been so bad I am not able to write. I got cold sleeping with the windows open all that hot weather and I have not been able to doo any thing but ride round. I got a few lines from John Richard [O. J.'s young son]. he had got my letter that I wrote at your house. Ruth earl and orricks Ruth was at Hariets yesterday. they did not go to see Adaline [Orrick's new wife]. Hariet has put up

three or 4 gallons of hackle burys or whortle burys write soon and
write a long letter. kiss Willie [6-months old] for me and constance
too we are going to have waffel cakes for super. we have a good time
today. no boddy here but us

your affectionate grandMother   M Hardgrove
give my best regard to Arther.
Henry has come but I have not saw him I have just come to town this
monday morning

Postscript: While it would be hard to believe this was the absolute final letter Margaret wrote, it is the last one saved. When she died, January 14, 1865, the war was almost over, and *The Massillon Independent* was only in its second year of publication. There was very little local coverage then. Obituaries, in those early newspaper pages, were rare. Hers read: "DIED— On the 14th inst. at the residence of Mr. Archer near Massillon. MARGARET HARDGROVE,[33] aged 68 years." After all those years of covering local news, Margaret's pen was stilled. If it surfaces some day in a box in an attic, it deserves to be in a place of honor in the McKinley Museum . . . beside other artifacts of these 3 Hardgrove family lines.

Some Come Home and Some Don't

The war ended, with its lingering surrender episodes, by the summer of 1865. That is when Hamilton's wife, Sabina, also picked up *her* pen. She wrote letters to her sister Mary back home in Pennsylvania. By that time, the couple was living in the southern part of Lawrence Township.[34] It was at a time when neighbors, like those in communities everywhere in Stark County, were rejoicing at the safe return of sons and husbands from the war; though, not every family had joyful homecomings. Some felt the sting of tending new graves in local cemeteries; others lived with sadness at never being able to visit graves of lost loved-ones. Also, not all families made it through the war in solid financial shape. Sabina was pregnant with her seventh child while the fifth one, Rachael, and sixth one, John Franklin Hardgrove, were still babies. Manners prohibited putting into writing any mention of that type of "confinement." In late spring, she had received letters from Mary saying that brother Jacob had just recently been killed. There was no news then about the homecoming of Jonathan "Joe" her youngest brother. Finally, one day in July, Sabina poured out her heart to Mary—a cathartic series of letters she wrote, not holding back, either, that she and Hamilton needed her father's help. Perhaps, she knew her sister could find the right moment to speak to their father, who was wracked with grief. And speak in a less emotional, less desperate way than she could manage to do, on paper. Here, now, is Sabina's and Hamilton's story, followed by her letters.

Sabina A. Strine was nearly 20 when she journeyed to Lawrence Township from Pennsylvania at the end of the 1840s to stay a while with her mother's brother, Uncle Jacob Giesaman,[35] in Ohio.

Traveling alone to Ohio was quite an adventure by stagecoach, stopping only to lodge, pick up passengers or take a meal. Jostling along in the coach and watching the country side pass by gave ample time to imagine how it would be staying with Uncle Giesaman and Aunt Anna. They also had a big family. Several daughters were Sabina's age, and she had corresponded with them. She had also heard news about their large farm through letters her mother had received. How different would life be away from home in Ohio? Only time would tell.

At first, she was a novelty in the household that already had its share of unique personalities. Matilda and Lavinia, the older girls, helped her settle in. While some of the younger children attended school, Sabina had the curious, littlest Giesamans following her as she blended into the family routine.

The months passed, and new social experiences presented themselves at church and among friends. It was not long until several young men made a point of stopping by the Giesaman's farm to visit Matilda, Lavinia and Sabina on Sunday afternoons. One of the them, Samuel Lucas, eventually asked to court Sabina.

Since Sam was already committed to farming and knew a lot of the Giesaman neighbors, they enjoyed exchanging experiences of growing up on farms—Sabina's large farm in Pennsylvania and Sam's farm in Ohio. After a short courtship and several letters exchanged with her parents back in Pennsylvania, Sam asked Sabina to marry him. Their minister presided over the wedding ceremony,[36] held several weeks before Christmas of 1848 in her aunt's and uncle's parlor. Sam was already working a farm in nearby Jackson Township,[37] and that evening, his neighbors welcomed the newlyweds home.

That winter they planned how they would work together to build up their farm.[38] And with hard work, it progressed from season to season. Nevertheless, it was an enormous shock when Sam died in 1851,[39] two summers after they were married.

So there she was, far away from immediate support from her close family. (Her mother had also died several years before that.) As a woman on her own, it took courage to keep moving

136

forward with settling affairs. (Wives were not automatically the beneficiary of their husband's property or possessions.)

One of the people who kept an eye on the very young Lucas widow in those early months was the skinny, lanky George Hamilton Hardgrove who was a life-long resident in Lawrence as well as cousin of the Butterbridge Hardgrove(s) and he had, at least, met Sam. In fact, sheep in Sam's herd had been bought from Rose Hardgrove's farm.[40] After meeting at various events, "Hamilton" asked Sabina if he could court her.

By late summer of 1853, Sabina and Hamilton agreed they wanted to build a life together and so were married by a Justice of the Peace in September.[41] In the next several years, the couple had four children.

In the early years, Hamilton worked as a laborer for several large farms in the countryside, south of Canal Fulton.[42] He also did some carpentry whenever the opportunity arose.

As the war continued year after year, far longer than anyone ever expected, community prayer events offered the only hope and solace for the end of the conflict and getting lives stabilized. Meanwhile, heroic initiative in "making-due" became a lifestyle. Households rationed sugar, butter and milk. Fresh coffee was a huge luxury not everyone could afford.[43] Illnesses were treated within the home as best they could, or in extreme cases, put "on the bill" with the local doctor.

For some, like Hamilton and Sabina, each day was a matter of praying and enduring. Sabina eventually heard that two of her brothers, Jacob and Jonathan G. Strine, had joined the service from Pennsylvania. Letters back and forth to Strine family members in Pennsylvania often experienced a delay in sharing news and could mainly relate just the surface of things, both in Lawrence Township and Pennsylvania.

Pvt. Jacob Strine[44]

Born October 26, 1838

Died April 2, 1865
Petersburg, VA
In Service of His Country
209th Reg., Penn., Co. D

July the 8 1865
Sabina Hardgrove

Dear sister it is a long time since i rote to you but is not
because i did not want to rite to you sooner. the letter was a
[great blow]to me i tell you to hear of my dear brother's
death. i thank God that you told me . . . not to hear from
him no more. Dear sister it seems hard but we will have to
bare with it . . . since i got your letter i tell you i have been

sick myself and after i got better two of my children took sick and was very sick. They got better and there was two more took down and we did not think that they would get well at all but they have. Now they are all beter than i am myself. It seems very hard but we will have to bare with it. I suppose that the rest of the family [six other married sisters and brothers] are all well. I want you to tell me now if Jonathan [youngest brother nicknamed "Joe" served 209th PA, "D" Co.] has got home and if he has is well. Tell him to come see us. The most of the boys has come home around us now and they are glad enough to get back again. [Time break.]

Dear Sister I have to change the subject for this time. I have not anything good to write. Things seem to be very hard with us and account of sickness it seems to mean that it cannot be that we must endure so much. All the time hamilton works by Day yet everything is so heigh yet they dont want to pay wages according with the rest of the things and us sick so much you can't make much a liven for such a large family as we have got. It makes me study pretty hard about home to think they dont try to help me a little when times is so hard. i think that papa might help me if he would give up a couple hundred dollars we could

*make a start on a farm again and then we could make a
good liven. But it is hard living this way. i have not had a
lot of food in the house for three months to eat. i want you
to tell John [eldest brother who did not enter the war] to
send me that money that he owes me so long. Tell him Tell
him that if ever I needed it it is now that i need it. i am here
all alone. i am here all alone poor and needy but no one
comes to my relief. i feel some times as though you have all
forsaken me when you all have plenty all the time you dont
think of poor me a way off all alone. If i have anything or
not you dont' know how hard it is. i want you to try and get
papa to do something for me if he can and i will be much
oblige to him for it. i want John to be sure to send me what
he owes me soon [No closing or signature.]*

March the 10 1866
Dear sister
*i this sabeth evening take up my pen to write a few lines to
you to let you know that i receive your most welcome letters
a few days ago and they found us all well at that time and
are all well at present excepting a very bad cold. Two of the
children had the cough since and have been very haurse
but have got better again. They are all better than i am*

140

myself. i dont feel very well but i dont expect to feel right *until i get over my scrafe witch i am looking for every day now. _____ will i ever get well or not only the lord knows. you stated in one of your letters that you was a coming to see me this sumer. i felt very much lifted up to think that you was coming and so was all the children. but when you rote and said that you could not come thair lips all fell and i was sorry to here the news myself for i thought i would once more get to see you. but diapointments is what i am used to in world but i hope and trust that father will not disapoint me this time in coming out this spring. i want him to come and bring me a lot of things. if you have lots of apple butter i want you to send me some for i cant get none here or dried apples or anything that you have got to spare to send me i will be very thankful to you for it. indeed we have hard geting along these hard times both in clothing and geting some thing to eat. if we had a little money we could do a little better to. it is hard doing any thing. i tell you i want you to try to get that money from John as soon as you can and send it to me if you please for i need it very bad. this war has set very hard on us . . . but i hope that times will be beter soon. if father comes out tell him to come to massilon on the express train and then take the frate at 2 oclock in the afternoon and come to lawrance [village eventually called North Lawrence]. that is only two miles from whare we live. John Hardgrove [Butterbridge Road cousin] lives rite in sight of lawrance. inquire for him he will bring you rite to our house being as we have no horse or buggy. and when you get to massilon you will have to stay thare from morning till 2 oclock. you inquire for Bennet Hardgrove [another Hardgrove cousin] and say thaire till the train comes out to lawrance. i will look for them strong.*

no more at present but i still remain your sister Sabina A Hardgrove rite as soon as you get this. i will send my picture as soon as i can

Postscript: Looking back on Sabina's and Hamilton's lives, as one does with the advantage of veiled, historical perspective, all indications (from lives of descendants) show that they must have received, at least, financial help from her father. What is known for sure is that she delivered her 7th baby, and they named him William Lincoln Hardgrove.[45]

Although Sabina was always very emotionally tied to family in Pennsylvania, she may or may not have had opportunity to take a train to visit them or ever again enjoy visits from them. At some point later in 1865, in-between her own letters to Mary, she likely received word that her brother Jonathan was wounded just before Jacob was killed. *(In fact, Jacob had been killed several days after saving Jonathan's life "on the battlefield.")*[46] Perhaps, they told her the serious extent of his injuries; or perhaps, they found it too exhausting (or horrific) to explain all that in writing.

Admittedly, it is mere conjecture that Hamilton, a carpenter, found jobs in the community of Lawrence, later called North Lawrence. New houses were being built and businesses were being established at that time—all happening on either side of the railroad tracks.[47] That much is clear. Another point is not.

In 21st century discussions of North Lawrence, many have argued that there "never was" a depot there. Sabina's letters prove, yes, during the Civil War the freight train stopped there and often carried passengers, as well. And one cannot stop hoping that, one fine day, Sabina's "Papa" stepped down onto that Lawrence platform.

EPILOGUE

John Henry Hardgrove married his sweetheart, Cordelia Razor, in the spring of 1865.[47] They lived in the heart of Massillon.[48] His plan to promote George Archer's patented hounds (an innovative approach to making covered wagons more secure for trips out West) apparently fell to obscurity; there is no proof he and George ever officially set up a bending business in Bucyrus. Perhaps it was due to the phasing-out of wagon and stage coach travel in favor of trains. "Henry" died while in his early 40's.

William and Ann remained a mere glimmer throughout the letters. They were busy with a good-size family ranging in ages from teen-agers to babies, yet *their letters* written to Margaret and Henry were a support throughout the Civil War. Fortunately, they saved much of Margaret's and Henry's correspondence, which was then passed along and treasured by family historian, Ruth Hardgrove Finch, a great-granddaughter of Margaret. (It was she who revealed that Margaret had beautiful dark auburn hair.) Ruth and family eventually worked to decipher and transcribe the letters in the 1940s or 50s. One hundred fifty years later, they will continue to guide genealogists and history buffs.

Orrick (O. J.) held onto the patent for the Horse Rake. He later went to Kansas and wrote extensive letters back to Butterbridge cousins about his lucrative blacksmith business and crops he grew on his farm. He died in Kansas, but it is believed his family later brought his body back to Stark County. One regret mentioned in his letters was that he could not get his son, John Richard, to join him in Kansas.[49] "Richard" stayed in Ohio and became a semi-pro baseball player. He was the first one to catch for the rookie, Cy Young.[50]

Minerva married Eugene Davenport, son of Joseph Davenport, who built railroad cars and invented the cow catcher for trains.[51] It is not surprising that Minerva and Eugene traveled to Kansas and resided near her brother Orrick for some years.[52] However, they later returned to the Massillon area. As an adult, she went by her middle name, Helen.

Mary Archer and her carriage-maker husband, George, continued to live on their farm in southwest Massillon. His iron hound invention (support for wagon masts) became less popular as railroad travel took over cross-country trips. Mary, herself, became known as a homeopathic doctor.[53]

Harriet Bahney and husband Hiram remained in Massillon and eventually had another son, whom they named O. J. The Bahney family had a prosperous furniture-making business and furniture store on South Erie Street.[54] A special item advertised in the 1860s was also being a dealer for Jenny Lind beds, popular during P. T. Barnum's sponsoring of the "Swedish Songstress," Jenny Lind.

George Hamilton Hardgrove was still the owner of property in Iowa when he died in 1889. Though there is no record that he and Sabina ever went there to see it, his name has been preserved on an early Iowa pioneer map.[55]

Sabina Strine Hardgrove spent her life raising 9 of her 10 children, losing Marshall when he was 13. In her life and in her death, however, she was also remembered for her strong faith.[56] Her granddaughter, Leafa Sabina Hardgrove McVay, was the first to relate a few specific details about the Hardgrove family which provided an initial seed for researching them.

Sources Consulted

1. Finch, Ruth, letter to Earl Kulgoski, 4 February 1965.
2. *Atlas of Stark County, Ohio*, (J. W. Beers & Co., 1870). 14.
3. *Commemorative Historical and Biographical Record of Wood County, Ohio; Its Past and Present.* (Indiana: J. H. Beers & Co., 1897). 1048-1049.
4. "*United States Census, 1850*," database with images FamilySearch (https://familysearch.org/ark:61903/1:1:MX76-GFT12 April 1016), John Hardgrove, Lawrence, Stark, Ohio, United States; citing family 378, NARA microfilm publication M432 (Washington, D. C.: National Archives and Records Administration, n. d.).
5. Powell, Esther, *Stark County Early Church Records, "Sarah J. Hardgrove, child of O. J. and Rachel," (Akron Historical Society, Self-pub., 1973). 195.*
6. Hostetler, Ned Eric. *The Railroad History of Orrville, Ohio* (Privately-pub., 1976). 3.
7. *Names in Stone,* John C. Hardgrove, Massillon City Cemetery (Find a Grave Memorial 93134463, 6 July, 2012).
8. Powell, Esther, *Stark County Early Church Records*, "Rachel Hardgrove, wife of O. J." 187.
9. "*United States Census, 1860*," database with images FamilySearch (https://familysearch.org/ark:61903/1:1:MCG1-4R6:12 April 2016), W Hardgrove, Brown Township, Knox, Ohio, United States; citing family 151, NARA microfilm publication M432.
10. *Massillon City Directory 1887-1888*, George Archer (Akron, Ohio: N. H. Burch & Co.). 29.
11. Williams, Albert B., ed., *Past and Present of Knox County, Ohio*, vol. 1. (Indianapolis: B. F. Bowen & Co., 1912). 294-295.
12. Crumrine, Boyd, ed., *The History of Washington County, Pennsylvania, with Biographical Sketches of Many of the Prominent Pioneers and Prominent Men* (Philadelphia: L. H. Evans, 1882). 496.

Sources Consulted

13. Thurston, Geo., H., compiler and pub., *Directory of the Monongahela and Youghiogheny Valleys: Containing Brief Historical Sketches Of The Various Towns Located On Them; With a Statistical Exhibit Of The Collieries Upon The Two Rivers* (Pittsburgh: A. A. Anderson, 1859). 83 and 60.
14. *"United States Census, 1850,"* database with images FamilySearch (https://familysearch.org/ark:/61903/ 1:1:MX76-GFK : 12 April 2016), Mitchell Hardgrove in household of Rose Hardgrove, Lawrence Township, Stark, Ohio, United States; citing family 376, NARA microfilm publication M432.
15. Hardgrove, Minnie, *Hardgrove Families* (North Lawrence, Ohio, 1934). 2.
16. Perrin, William Henry, ed., *History of Stark County, With Outline Sketches of Ohio* (Chicago: Baskin & Battey, 1881). 453.
17. Hardgrove, Richard, *Estate Sale Log* (1843).
18. *Founding of Justus.* (Brewster Sugar Creek Township Historical Society). 2-3.
19. Hardgrove, Minnie, *Hardgrove Families* (1934). 1.
20. *Funeral Eulogy notes*, Mary Hardgrove Sheaffer (February 1905).
21. *Funeral Eulogy notes,* Mary Hardgrove Sheaffer (February 1905).
22. "Married—Mr. Mitchell Hardgrove and Miss Hannah Justus," *Canton Repository*, 7 March 1860, 3, col. 2.
23. Hardgrove, Willy, date of birth: 4 January, 1861, Massillon City Cemetery records.
24. Mrs. M. Hardgrove, Interred 13 January, 1861, Massillon City Cemetery.
25. "United States Census, 1860," data base with images, FamilySearch.(hpps://familysearch.org/ark:/ 61903/1:1:MCPW-6BQ:13 December 2017), Mary A. Archer in entry for George Archer, Tuscarawas Township, Stark, Ohio, United States; citing family 1958, NARA Microfilm publication M653. 270.
26. Hardgrove, Willy, son of M. Hardgrove, died 11 October

Sources Consulted

26. (*Continued*) 1861, Massillon City Cemetery records.
27. Hostetler, Ned Eric, *The Railroad History of Orrville, Ohio* (Privately-pub., 1976). 16.
28. L. O. Weiss, *Orrville Yesterday & Today* (Self-pub. 1965). 87.
29. "*United States Census, 1860*," data base with images, FamilySearch (hpps://familysearch.org/ark:/1 :1:MCLY-WPC: 26 July 2017), Chas Eckert, Lawrence Township, Stark, Ohio, United States; citing family 207, NARA Microfilm publication M653. 236.
30. McVay, Leafa Sabina Hardgrove, Personal communication with Kathryn Hardgrove Popio, May 1975.
31. *Massillon City Directory 1887-1888*, George Archer. 29.
32. Union Cemetery tombstone, Mitchell H. Hardgrove, Canal Fulton, Ohio.
33. "DIED—On the 14th at the residence of Mr. Archer near Massillon, Margaret Hardgrove, aged 68 years," *Massillon Independent*, 19 January, 1865, 2, col.4.
34. "United States Census, 1870," data base with images, FamilySearch (https://FamilySearch.org/ark:61903/1:1:M6LR-RFB:12 April 2016), George Hardgrove, Lawrence Township, Ohio; citing family 191, NARA microfilm publication M593.
35. "United States Census, 1860," data base with images, FamilySearch (https://FamilySearch.org/ark:/61903/1:1:MX76-C97: 12 April 2016), Jacob Gieseman, Lawrence, Stark, Ohio, United States; citing family 355, NARA microfilm publication M432.
36. "Ohio Marriages, 1800-1958," database, FamilySearch (https://familysearch.org/ark:/61903/1:1:XDKV-LX2: 8 December 2014), Samuel Lucas and Sabina Strine, 11 Dec 1848; citing Star, Ohio, reference:FHL microfil 0897628 V. A-C.
37. Richard Hardgrove Estate Sale log (1843).
38. "United States Census, 1850," data base with images, FamilySearch (https://familysearch.org/ark:/61903/1:1:mx76-WX5: 12 APRIL 2016), Saml Lucas, Jackson,

Sources Consulted

38. (*Continued*) Stark, Ohio, United States; citing family 263, NARA microfilm publication M432.
39. "Find a Grave," database, FamilySearch (https://family-search.org/ark:/61903/1:1:QVLY-63HV: 13 December 2015), Samuel Lucas, 1851; Burial, Stark, Ohio, United States of America, Newman Cemetery; citing record ID 104485721.
40. Bill of Property Sold By Dougal Campbell, Administrator of the Estate of Richard Hardgrove, deceased, at public auction (15 December 1843).
41. Marriage Registration Book, Stark County Court House, Canton, Ohio (1980).
42. "United States Census, 1860," (https://familysearch.org/ark:/61903/1:1:MCLY-WPC : 26 July 2017), Chas Eckert.
43. Hunt, Irene, *Across Five Aprils* (Chicago: Follett Publishing Company, 1984). 65.
44. Strine, Jacob, Strine Family Genealogy. 137-141.
45. "United States Census, 1880," data base with images, FamilySearch (https://familysearch.org/ark:61903/1:1: MCLY-WPC: 26 July 2017), George Hardgrove, Lawrence Township, Stark, Ohio, United States; citing family 207, NARA microfilm publication M653.236.
46. Strine, Jacob and Jonathan G., Family Genealogy. 137-141.
47. Perrin, William Henry, ed., *History of Stark County, With Outline Sketches of Ohio* (Chicago: Baskin & Battey, 1881). 142.
48. "Ohio Marriages, 1800-1856," data base, FamilySearch (February 2018, John H Hardgrove and Cordelia E. Razor, 27 April 1865); citing Stark, Ohio, reference; FHL microfilm 1897629. V. 5-6.
49. "United States Census, 1870," data base with images, (FamilySearch. org/ark:/61903/1:1:M6VY-FFB: 12 April 2016), J H Hardgrove, Ohio, United States; citing p. 20, family 154, NARA microfilm publication M593.
50. O. J. Hardgrove, letter to Wm. Hardgrove (Wm. Martin Hardgrove in Lawrence Township), 26 April 1880.
51. "Akronite Caught Cy Young in First Game," *The Akron Times Press,*" 10 March 1928. 1.

Sources Consulted

52. Pond, Mandy Altimus, *Images of America, Early Massillon and Lost Kendall* (Charleston: Arcadia Publishing Company, 2017). 59.
53. O. J. Hardgrove, letter to Wm. Hardgrove (William Martin Hardgrove of Lawrence Township), 26 April 1880.
54. Finch, Ruth, letter to Earl Kulgoski, 4 February, 1965.
55. "Dealer in Jenny Lind," *Massillon Independent*, July 10, 1863. Ad, page 2.
56. Plat of Homer, Buchanan County, Iowa, (Minneapolis: Warner & Foote, 1886). 7.
57. "Prayer For Health But Swift-winged Death Stopped Not Its Flight," *Massillon Independent*, February 12, 1899.

INDEX

INDEX

Canton, Ohio (cont.)
123, 126
Chickhominy (Battle on the) 84
Cincinnati, Ohio, 62, 81
Cincinnati Daily Commercial,
63, 106
Clapper, Margaret M., 39
Clapper, Rosey, 39
Clapper, Sally, 49
Clemons, Jo, 60, 61
Columbiana Co., 21-22
Columbus, Ohio, 70, 94, 117
Connellsville, Pennsylvania, 3
"Copperheads," 105, 111
Corinth (Mississippi), 25, 26, 27,
31, 33, 36, 41, 49, 51, 69,
73
Cotton, Doctor, 10
Culpepper Court House 117
Curtis, Samuel Ryan, 80
Dayly Com (Daily), 107, 126
Davenport, Joseph, 52, 54-55, 144
Davis, Jefferson (Jeff), 56
Deans (family), 55, 108
Division: Wallace, 25
Dixie (Dixsee), 55, 99
Dolly Dutten Concert, 106
Dover, Tennessee, 49
Downs, Curtis, 4
Downs, Mary Ann, 102
Doxey, Isaac, 31, 78, 92, 121
Earl, George, 7, 13, 26, 37, 53, 64,
80, 82, 87, 107, 110, 113, 121
Earl, Gilberthorp, 8, 53, 64, 113,
121, 131, 132
Earl, Ruth Hardgrove, 7, 64, 107,
109, 113 121, 131, 132, 133
Eckert, Adaline, 29
Eckert, Charles, 29
Eckert, David, 29
Eckert, Ellen, 29
Edgar, Joe (Jo), 79
Everhart, Rachel, 108

Falk, Mrs., 108
Firestone (family), 102
Floyed: (Re: Ft. Donelson), 47
Foltz, 78
Ford, Tom, 86
Fort Donelson, 32, 39, 48, 56, 90
Fort Pickering, 57
Fort Pillow, 94
Fort Sumter, 23
Frasher, Mrs. Lu, 111
Fredericksburg, Ohio, 99, 102
Giesaman, Jacob & Anna, 135, 136
Giesaman, Lavinia, 136
Giesaman, Matilda, 136
Grant, Ulysses S., 89
Hall, Selina, 23, 24, 121
Halsted, Clara, 113, 114, 116
Hardgrove, Adaline, 133
Hardgrove, Ann (daughter), 9,
34, 84, 85, 99, 123
Hardgrove, Bennet, 30, 31, 39, 50,
78, 100, 142
Hardgrove, Betsey, 35, 37, 39, 107
Hardgrove, Constance, 10, 36, 93,
127, 134
Hardgrove, Dick (John Richard),
35, 62, 103, 127, 132, 133
Hardgrove, Eleanor Jane, 29
Hardgrove, Emila, 29
Hardgrove, George, 7, 8, 132
Hardgrove, (George) Hamilton, 28,
29, 30, 37, 135, 137, 139, 143
Hardgrove, Hannah Justus, 8, 12
Hardgrove, John M., 7, 31, 37, 92,
142
Hardgrove, John Crawford, 3
Hardgrove, John Franklin, 135
Hardgrove, Henry, 21, 25, 26
Hardgrove, John Henry, 3, 5, 10,
11-12, 13, 15-19, 21-23, 25-
28, 30, 31, 32-34, 35, 36- 37,
42-49, 50, 51, 53, 54-61, 63,
64, 65, 666, 68-74, 76-78,

152

INDEX

INDEX

154

INDEX